libd

D0559348

THE BOLLINGEN SERIES XVI

T. W

# Lectures in Criticism

THE JOHNS HOPKINS UNIVERSITY

*R. P. Blackmur · Benedetto Croce · Henri M. Peyre*
*John Crowe Ransom · Herbert Read · Allen Tate*

Introduction by Huntington Cairns

BOLLINGEN SERIES XVI

PANTHEON BOOKS

Randall Library UNC-W

COPYRIGHT 1949 BY BOLLINGEN FOUNDATION INC., NEW YORK, N. Y.

PUBLISHED FOR BOLLINGEN FOUNDATION INC.

BY PANTHEON BOOKS INC.

MANUFACTURED IN THE U.S.A.

PRINTED BY THE MARCHBANKS PRESS, N. Y.

PN
85
.L4

# Table of Contents

# FOREWORD

WITH a view toward reassessing the place of literary criticism in our day, as well as the task and obligation of the literary critic, the Department of Writing, Speech, and Drama of The Johns Hopkins University conceived the idea of sponsoring a symposium on the great critics of the past. The immediate object was a fresh examination of some of the salients in the history of critical judgment. It was hoped that new light and direction might thereby be afforded contemporary criticism. Among the critics chosen for re-examination were Aristotle, Longinus, Coleridge, and De Sanctis, and it was thought advisable also to provide specifically for a discussion of present problems.

Designated as The Johns Hopkins University Lectures in Criticism, the lectures took place in Baltimore, in April, 1948. Of the essays included in this volume, all were delivered at the symposium. Signor Croce was unable to be present; his lecture was read by Francis J. Thompson of The Johns Hopkins University. Dr. Isaiah Bowman, President of the University, made the opening remarks. Huntington Cairns, of the National Gallery of Art, presided at the formal meetings and at the symposia which followed.

*Grateful acknowledgment is herewith made to the authors of these papers, whose generous response to the invitation of the University made possible this contribution to an understanding and appreciation of the function of criticism.*

ELLIOTT COLEMAN
Chairman, Department of
Writing, Speech, and Drama
The Johns Hopkins University

x

# INTRODUCTION

FROM the beginning criticism has exhibited two aspects. In one it has compared and judged; it has attempted to isolate the values of literature and to determine whether the specimens it appraises are good or bad. This has been a continuing function of criticism from the days when the sixth century B.C. discovered that Homer was immoral and should not be read, to T. S. Eliot's pronouncement that the last canto of the *Paradiso* represents the highest point that poetry has reached or ever can reach. In its other aspect, criticism does not seek to judge but to explain. It sees literature as a whole, or in an adequate segment; it purports to discover a significant problem lying in the area under examination; and it offers a theory to account for the difficulty. This also has been a continuing view of criticism from the earliest times. It finds expression in Homer's doctrine that the end of poetry is pleasure, as well as in the current insistence upon close textual reading as the key to the discovery of meaning. Each of these aspects of criticism presents a difficulty that the labors of all the generations of critics have not resolved. Until such embarrassments are overcome criticism will continue to manifest the confusion it has always shown.

As Kant observed, the critic will not infrequently defend his judgment with the assertion that it is merely subjective, and will readily admit that it therefore does not necessarily command the agreement of others. However, even those who say that the grounds of the judgment are objective, and hence binding on everyone, agree that the determining considerations cannot be reduced to definite principles. Thus, it is possible to argue about the validity of a judgment, but not to determine the question by proof, since no principles have been agreed upon. But to admit that it is legitimate to argue about judgments is to assert the contrary of the proposition that judgments are subjective. On this basis Kant constructed his antinomy of taste: thesis — the judgment of taste is not based upon principles, for, if it were, it could be determined by proofs; antithesis — the judgment of taste is based on principles, for otherwise, notwithstanding our lack of agreement, we would not be attempting to persuade each other of the validity of our own judgments.

However, the antinomy grants too much; it permits the subjective critic to have his cake and to eat it. He can argue that there are no standards except his own feelings, so long as it is to his advantage to do so. When the same position is asserted by others to his disadvantage, he can promptly find standards from which to deduce that his opponents do not know their business. Balzac, for George Moore, displayed greater imaginative power than Shakespeare. This judgment, he admitted easily, was only the expression of an individual taste, and interesting so far as it revealed to the reader the different developments and progress of Moore's mind. But a critic who ventured, on the same ground, to class Scott with Balzac was regarded with pity by Moore. He thought that such a judgment would have drawn only blank stares from Virgil, Horace, and Catullus, who lived in an age of standards, and, furthermore, that such an opinion could be held only by one whose views had been corrupted by Christianity.

Actually, the subjective judgment is not a judgment, but an autobiographical statement. It has the form of a judgment, but it does not report on a value of literature; it reports on a feeling of the critic. When the subjective critic asserts, "*Hamlet* is a great play," all he means, if he denies the existence of standards, is that he experiences an emotional approval on reading *Hamlet;* he makes no assertion with respect to the existence of any literary quality attributable to *Hamlet* which has even the possibility of ascertainment by another critic, since the approval means only that it is approved emotionally by the critic himself. Autobiographical statements of this kind are not without interest to criticism. Arthur Symons' account of his feelings on witnessing *Antony and Cleopatra,* and Anatole France's comparable narrative after viewing *Hamlet,* contain material which literary critics have put to important use. But personal histories of that kind do not belong to the aspect of literary criticism which renders judgment; they are a part of the criticism that is concerned with the problematic aspect of literature. Either literary criticism must give judgment on some basis other than the purely autobiographical one, or it should cease altogether to pretend that it possesses the capacity to perform the function of judgment.

To hold otherwise is to encounter the difficulties that meet subjectivist theories of value generally, namely: the judgment can never be erroneous unless the critic is misrepresenting his own emotions; Mr. Eliot's view that Coleridge was a good critic and Mr. Lucas' view that he was a bad one are not logically contradictory; all evidence brought forward to support a subjective judgment or overturn that of another critic is irrelevant, except evidence bearing on the personal feelings of the critic. For literary criticism, in the face of these absurdities, to attempt to hold to the autobiographical view and, at the same time, claim to be able to render judgment, is a logical impossibility.

Literary criticism must thus pass over wholly into its problematic functions, and abandon altogether the giving of judgment, or it must ground its judgments on something other than the emotional approval of the critic. The first task that confronts literary criticism, if it wishes to correct its present chaotic condition, is to determine whether it can give valid judgments or not. It can only do that by formulating propositions in terms of which literature should be judged, and endeavoring to ascertain whether those propositions are consistent, whether they have been properly deduced from other propositions, whether they support the judgments which it is asserted follow from them, and by otherwise testing them. If a program of this sort is not followed, it is difficult to perceive how criticism in one of its traditionally most important aspects has any proper subject matter at all.

This view allows for the possibility that the qualities that the critic discovers in literature are valuable for their own sake and not because they are approved by the critic, but that nevertheless, because they are unique, no account can be given of them. That is to say, we can recognize beauty just as we can recognize color, but we can describe neither of them. This theory at once raises the question of how we know when we are in the presence of beauty, since no one can describe it to us. The customary answer, from Plato to Bertrand Russell, has been that we know it through inherent knowledge. However that may be, the theory admits that critics are talking about values which can be considered in their own right, and that their assertions involve something more than an account of the condition of their own feelings.

Each age has given us the proposition which it felt lay behind valid literary judgment. Perhaps some of the most important are Plato's doctrine that the work of art must have an organic unity, that its elements must be as interrelated as the elements of a living organism; Aristotle's theory that poetry is a concrete expression of the universal, and that the primary end of poetry is to give pleasure; the insistence of Horace upon the importance of tradition; the Longinian view that literature has its own qualities of importance alto-

scope as Saintsbury's, is, nevertheless, within its limits, an attempt to cover both aspects of the field. It is no doubt a coincidence that the very time of the publication of Saintsbury's *History* — the turn of the century — can be taken as the moment when the main effort of criticism shifted from judgment to explanation.

Criticism in its explanatory aspect faces the same difficulty that all branches of inquiry must overcome: it has to learn to ask the right questions. Like a child digging for shells at the seashore, criticism, for the whole of its history, has put its questions haphazardly, in the hope that something important would turn up.

If we take Aristophanes as the first important critic in Western literature we find him raising the question: In what order of merit shall the poets be ranked, and on what basis? Aeschylos is assigned first place, and the tests are technical skill (δεινότης) and wise counsel (νουθεσία) that will improve citizenship. Is this the kind of question that criticism ought to ask? Probably no one with any critical perception would affirm today that the placing of poets in a one, two, three order is helpful. Its sterility is visible to us in many examples of Greek and Latin criticism. Mr. Gilbert Murray tries to save the question by rewriting it in the following form: The world seems empty of poetry; if we could bring back from Hades one poet and only one, would it be Euripides, or are there greater poets still? At best this seems to transform the question into nothing more than a

harmless parlor game; any answer to it would possess about
as much critical validity as Taine's remark, *"J'aime mieux
Alfred de Musset,"* as a criticism of Tennyson. But Aristophanes was not altogether on the wrong track. A critic like
Saintsbury, wedded to the comparative method, could (and
did) ask himself: Can I relate the writer to his time and
country, to language and manner, to predecessors and successors, not with the aim of determining his rank, but of dis-
engaging his qualities? The bulk of the effort of twentieth-
century criticism has been devoted precisely to the attempt
to answer that question.

With Plato a different type of question was asked: What
is the prime function of poetry? Plato's answer — to disclose the beauty of the world — is supported by elaborate
dialectical and empirical considerations. With the literature that Plato had before him, it was perhaps the only possible answer; it breaks down for us because it will not fit
the facts of Western poetry. It is a type of question that is
concerned as little as possible with the giving of judgment;
it is the type of question that the twentieth-century critic is
most likely to ask himself. Mr. Blackmur's "What is the relationship between form and value?," Mr. Ransom's "Can
form in poetry be sacrificed to self-expression?," and Mr.
Peyre's "Has criticism as it is practiced anything of value
to offer the creative writer?" are all the great-grandchildren
of Plato's inquiry.

It was Bacon who first observed that to ask the right question is the half of knowledge, a maxim that he underscored when he insisted that science begins when man starts "putting Nature to the question," *i.e.*, to the torture. Science was thus not a matter of merely collecting facts, classifying them, and then allowing them to speak for themselves. Since Kant used a quotation from Bacon on the title page of the *Critique of Pure Reason* this has suggested a new view of that learned volume to a recent clever interpreter. Kant saw that progress in physics and mathematics was due to the fact that workers in those fields put the proper questions and demanded satisfactory answers. They gave up looking for facts and asking what they proved; instead, they framed hypotheses and tested them by experiments. The moral for Kant was that metaphysics should also put its questions in a fit manner, and not in the chaotic fashion that had hitherto prevailed. The whole of the *Critique* can therefore be regarded as an attempt to tell metaphysicians what kind of questions they should ask.

Criticism is still without its Kant, but its own history contains ample warnings of the dangers which accompany the putting of futile or misleading questions. Here its principal task is to determine whether the questions it asks point to a genuine problem. Those questions must not be *questions frivoles,* as Condillac called them; because they have too often been of that kind each generation has had to devise what it calls the new criticism. How to determine that criticism is not asking trifling questions is no easy task for the

generation that first propounds them. Perhaps the first requirement is to ask only questions to which the inquirer
believes he has the answer; and the second, to know fairly
well how to extract an answer that will satisfy others.
Acton's injunction, "Study problems, not periods," is as
fruitful a guide for criticism as for history. The rub is that
he told no one how to avoid asking silly questions.

All this is to say that criticism for twenty-three hundred
years has lacked a volume which might have begun:

> *Our subject is criticism, and I propose to speak not
> only of the art in general, but also of the various kinds
> and their respective capacities; of the principles re-
> quired for good criticism; and whatever else is proper
> to this same inquiry. Let us follow the natural order
> and begin first with first principles. . . .*

These words, alas, are not the opening words of a *Kritike*
by Aristotle — a περὶ κριτικῆς τέχνης that organized criticism as the *Poetics* did poetry. It is pleasant to speculate upon what Aristotle's *Kritike* might have accom-
plished. Like its companion volume it would, no doubt, have
been brief, tough-minded, and bold in content. It would
have mediated the conflicts of earlier critics, and added its
own confident insights. We might expect that it would be
reprinted more often than any other Greek volume except
the New Testament, and that it would inspire some Burke
to observe that it makes further discourse upon the subject

the less necessary. Above all, it would have stated the theory of criticism in a form of the utmost generality, but one which would, nevertheless, allow the future to add to or subtract from it as the novelties of creative activity indicated. Criticism has always stood in need of such a *Kritike*, and no more so than at the present. Any inquiry into the bases of criticism is always a prolegomenon to such an undertaking.

HUNTINGTON CAIRNS

*John Crowe Ransom*

# THE LITERARY CRITICISM
# OF ARISTOTLE

*John Crowe Ransom*

# THE LITERARY CRITICISM
# OF ARISTOTLE

IF THERE were a subtitle, I should like it as follows: the literary criticism of a man of letters who had become a pedagogue, and of an idealist who had become a naturalist.

We are present upon an academic occasion, at which it is an honor to assist. Let me begin by recalling a handsome consideration which is cited by intellectual historians. The Lyceum which Aristotle founded late in life, and directed for thirteen years, was the first university to exist according to the pattern that Europeans and Americans now know so familiarly. The Aristotle with whom we are acquainted is the Aristotle of the Lyceum, an academic man, dedicated to a career of oral teaching, despiteful of the glory which awaits the literary man, and, as I think the saying goes in the administrative offices of the modern academy, "unproductive" in the public sense. What he left to posterity was the ferment of his ideas in the heads of his old pupils, plus the lecture notes from which he had taught them, and which some of them might edit and publish later if they liked. (No mention is made of these notebooks in the author's will,

which as such documents go is a model of modesty as well
as kindly personal consideration.) The *Rhetoric* and the
*Poetics* contain his literary criticism, and both have precisely this history: they are Aristotle's private lecture notes.

We feel an irony when we reflect that the idealistic Plato
never overcame his intellectual distaste for the "world of
appearances," which was nothing else but this actual and
sensible world, yet gave to his public writing such a literary
beauty as subsequent philosophers have not repeated. We
may be very sure that every literary stroke of Plato's pen
bears testimony to the fascinating configurations of this
world. We are glad of his condescension, for it relieves us
of what might have been the impression of a poverty of substance greater than we could bear. On the other hand, it was
Aristotle's part to emerge slowly from Plato's ambitious
and puritanical discipline, and undertake to point the human
career to such happiness as the ample natural world provides; yet he had the identical inconsistency of Plato, only
in reverse. He turned from the stiff Platonic doctrines, and
also from the literary form of the stiff Platonic dialogue, in
spite of some brilliant early successes with it, and was content to seek and tell the specific, the naked truth. This is a
man whom I must hold in extraordinary honor. Yet his habit
of delivery is not that of the literary critic according to our
own convention. What is more important, at that stage in the
thinking of Europe, the time for a mature theory of literature had not arrived, so that in his own theory we have much

of solid rightness, but at crucial places it goes along with a scantness, almost a willful withholding, as in the deliverances of the oracle of Delphi — indicating hard labor for the interpreters.

A schoolmaster's literary criticism cannot be quite the thing we now find ourselves coveting. There is a criticism which is literary in the double sense; the literary quality attaches to the object of criticism of course, but it attaches to the work of criticism too. The indubitable art work invites a low-grade and lesser art work to celebrate as well as judge it. The critic never ceases to be impressed with his fine object. He starts with a spontaneous surge of piety, and is inducted by the contagion of art into a composition of his own, which sustains the warmth unashamed, and probably manages a rounded literary effect, having a beginning, a middle, and an end. All that is delightful, it is what we need, it must be according to the deepest proprieties. But the procedure is likely to seem unprofessional to the academic critic, for it is his virtue to have made the choice of Aristotle, and to be seeking but the one thing: to deliver the critical judgment with justice and precision.

On the other side, there are advantages for us in the academic commodity. And the first one is that the academic man, at least if his scruple is of Aristotelian grade, does not shake several bushes at once and confuse the categories, but attends to one category at a time. That is the way to obtain definitive findings. Today we shall spend our time on the

*Poetics*, waiving the *Rhetoric*; and on that larger part of the *Poetics* which deals with tragedy, waiving the part about epic, and not speculating as to the part about comedy, which is missing. So let us first remark that Aristotle does not mix the literary or poetic issues of drama with its moral issues; I had almost said, does not adulterate them. He could have discoursed about morals if he had liked, and with what we are tempted to call an Aristotelian authority, which here was very great; the tragic heroes are morally above the average, as he says, while their moral consciousness is acute; but it is also vocal, and articulate, easily to be taken by the critic at its face value, and that is not the thing which makes the heroes' delivery poetical; if it is the thing which makes it moral, still this is the *Poetics*, not the *Ethics* according to Eudemos or according to Nikomachos. Nor does he indulge in religious theory under color of discussing poetic theory. It is always commented that he never mentions what must have been even more familiar to his public than to us: the fact that the Attic tragedies originated in the holy festival of Dionysos. If they were full of allusions to judgments that ubiquitous Greek gods passed upon offending heroes, and heroines, these must have seemed symbolic determinations to Aristotle, whose naturalistic cast of thought was always gaining upon his transcendental training; and since the natural world, to all intents and purposes, means "everything in the world," it is certainly well provided with sequences, and consequences, which even the hero's strength is not going to controvert; these will take their course, they will humble his spirit sufficiently for anybody's taste, and if he is a hero the sign is that he will accept them with a certain style, which his poet will know how to render. Aristotle got the tragedies into simpler dramatic perspective by secularizing them, naturalizing them. Do religious persons find that the tragedies have thereby been robbed of their religious interest? That would be odd. We must stop on that a moment; Aristotelianism, the naturalistic way of thinking, is at stake. The movement from ritual to romance, and from romance to naturalism, seems to be according to the line of the human progress, and perhaps on the whole the line can be traversed in only one direction. Doubtless this is just about as bad as it is good. But it is a linguistic phenomenon; a matter of translating from an earlier language into a later. In the course of this translation nothing that is valid need be given up for lost, for the value was always that of a symbol whose referent was something that "took place" in the natural world.

There is another advantage in the criticism which comes out of the academy, a double one. The area of literary judgment has two margins, which might be called a nether margin and an upper, and there is always a good deal of exploration to be done in both the marginal areas. Let the nether area be the one to which the academic man devotes his professional "scholarship." He must be learned in the culture and language of the period, the biography of the author, the bibliography of the works, and all that, which could easily be rehearsed on some other academic occasion. It is enough that Aristotle was of exemplary erudition, and prodigious in research. It was he who recovered to the Greek world the list of the tragic trilogies which had taken the three prizes in each of the years since the time of Aeschylos, when this Apollonian entertainment, which Aristotle liked very much, had come to follow upon the primitive Dionysian revels, which could not have been much to his taste. The list had a coverage of many hundreds of single plays. Nor is there any doubt that he knew the plays, if the texts were still available, and the illustrations in the *Poetics* cite many which are unknown to us. Our own stock is of about thirty tragedies, all by Aeschylos, Sophocles, and Euripides, out of about two hundred and fifty which are ascribed to these authors alone. Incidentally, they have great individual differences for us, yet belong so uniformly to a single genre, highly perfected and sustained over an almost unbelievable period in a changeful age, that we know we do not run a big risk, nor are the first to run it, if we judge that our critic was lecturing upon what is still the finest national achievement in our Western literature. He had his data in hand.

At the other margin of critical judgment we enter a speculative region. Here the academic critic must furnish a philosophical equipment. Aristotle's was the kind of naturalistic philosophy which inquires into functions or final causes. What is poetry good for, if it claims a place in the crowded psychic economy? What passion have we in mind if we profess a passionate concern with poetry? As the race becomes increasingly self-conscious, that is to say philosophical, and psychological, we require the fine behaviors as well as the gross or common ones to disclose their human significance, and we include the behavior of reverence, which is religious, and the behavior of seeking and sensing beauty, which is aesthetic.

Now we have come to the essential synoptic shape of the thought of Aristotle the critic. You will have anticipated me. We must figure *mimesis* or imitation, and *katharsis* or purgation, and I do not doubt that the reporter will stand or fall according as he pronounces upon these cardinal Aristotelian usages.

Imitation is Plato's mocking term for the poetic procedure as compared with what he regarded as better procedures. Aristotle took it over without remark as a correct technical description. It is the use of language to denote natural objects as given, contingent, today as "existential"; to be received in their fullness, which is their givenness; to be distinguished from those abstract or working objects that we employ in practical operations without having to notice them except to see whether they answer to the specifications we have laid down. And the peculiar linguistic device which accomplishes this feat is a kind of mimicry; Aristotle cites for example the picture which conveys the object through a configuration of lines on the paper just like the object's own.

Mimicry is strictly a human gift, but it is scarcely affected
with magical powers or metaphysical ones. In the literary
art, the words are mimetic indirectly; they evoke images of
the natural objects, and the images are mimetic. And there
is no great trick to that. But let us enforce the term beyond
possible misunderstanding. We are speaking mimetic or
poetic language, we are evoking the whole or natural object,
the moment we qualify the common noun by a single adjective or association which is not contained in its definition.
To take a homely illustration, we hear that a lady has gone
to the butcher's with her shopping basket. We know what a
butcher is: a species of economic agent with whom house-
wives deal, the instances being indifferent, i.e. one just like
another, unless perhaps they may have been graded, and
given numerical coefficients to indicate their economic rat-
ings. But suddenly it is said that the lady finds her butcher
*slumped over his chopping-block and weeping;* immediately
we are transported into a world of contingencies, surprises,
local excitements, possible dangers, more intractable than
we were prepared for. That is an ambiguous example, since
it may lead to action or to aesthetic contemplation. A literary
example, which involves the technical device of figure of
speech and is cited by Aristotle under the head of poetic
diction, is where Aeschylos represents Philoctetes as saying
of his ancient wound: "The ulcer eats the flesh of this foot
of mine." And Euripides, altering things as usual to his
taste, stretches the figure and has Philoctetes say: "The ulcer

is feasting upon my foot." The common situation turns
exotic, and vivid. One poet casually makes the ulcer into a
devouring monster. The other poet says to himself that we
may not choose to see it so, for we have had it put this way
before — for example, Aristotle's own father, the physician,
might carelessly have remarked that some ulcer was "eat-
ing" into the flesh — but he will compel us, so he turns the
monster into a decadent Corinthian epicure making a ban-
quet on flesh he should never have eaten. But a third example
is needed to show the gentle side of the tragic imagery,
though the English translation is execrable. It is where the
unhappy Trojan women listen to the lamentation which fills
their ruined city. But the object is too large and obsessive
for them, and their sensibility must be freshened, and gen-
tled, so that a humble image from bird life is imported:

> *The sea-washed shores around*
> *With cries and shrieks resound,*
> *As when the poor bird for her young complains,*
> *And anguish swells her strains.*

The technique always works by citing some excess of natural
quality which removes the object from classification and
disposition, as a particular always qualitatively exceeds the
universal. I labor this a little, but the distinction is crucial.
Without the excess, which is not every time though perhaps
normally a "fine" excess, the particular collapses into the
familiar universal, the language of imitation returns to the
language of logic and use.

But what is the service of these imitations? What do we want with objects realized in their fullness when the uses of the appetitive life are satisfied with any objects that meet the respective qualifications, and the excess of the proper noun over the common noun comes to us, if we are attending to our own business, as an inordinate claim upon our attention? Aristotle had his answer to these questions, but at first sight it comes close to quibbling. Thus: we value an imitation because it gives us pleasure. That is almost a tautology. If we ask somebody, Why do you do this? and he replies, Because I like to do it, we are offended, feeling that we knew as much already. But in strictness Aristotle's answer is not a tautology. Frequently he remarked, though perhaps not in the *Poetics*, that we do some things for no other reason than the pleasure of doing them, and these activities are ends in themselves; but do other things which are laborious and painful, not pleasant at all, because they are the means to pleasure eventually. Therefore when he says that we value imitation because of the intrinsic pleasure, he means that there is no ulterior reason. It is the first occurrence so far as I know of the doctrine of art for art's sake. Yet Aristotle as a naturalist ought never to stop being concerned with ulterior reasons. Plato said readily enough that poetic imitation was pleasant, but argued that this was a vicious pleasure, and ought not to be indulged, since its consequence was vulgarizing, and discouraging to real intellectual attainment. Aristotle does not seriously take up that argument. Putting the best construction upon his silence, we may say that he is a good naturalist insofar as he accepts on principle all the staple behaviors of the species, not rejecting some because they are considered vulgar but thinking that their human universality presents them in compelling dignity. Yet a modern naturalist cannot stop there. He does not believe for a moment in isolated faculties, in behaviors that have no relation to the general psychic economy. The notion of a behavior for the behavior's sake is not one that a post-Darwinian naturalist, for example, will entertain; for I think it must be a postulate of the doctrine of biological evolution that within the evolved species every established pattern of activity, whether psychological or physiological, is one which has proved its case as a true organic function. With all his genius, Aristotle was unacquainted with Darwin. But just as a special salvation has to be arranged by Christian theologians for Abraham and the heroes of the Old Testament, so we must have a saving clause for Aristotle the pre-Darwinian naturalist. Let it be only for modern poetic theorists that we denounce art for art's sake as an evasive slogan, an abrogation of biological responsibility. Unless, of course, it should happen to be a mere Bohemian brashness, to tease the moralists with; and we will not make a quarrel with the wits.

But the doctrine became difficult of application when Aristotle must pass upon the specific art of Attic tragedy. The intrinsic pleasure would seem insignificant there. It is true that the poetic imitations keep going at the usual rate, on the periphery so to speak of the principal action, as if the poet were saying to the dramatist, "My show must go on too." But what is their force against the human sufferings portrayed in the tragic action, heightened steadily, protracted clear to the moment of death, which is the obscene stroke itself, and must not be included directly in the action but only reported, or rendered by a noise from the wings, offstage? Aristotle insists, of course, that the little pleasures, which luxuriate in the poetic diction, are there to be received, though he maintains brazenly that the tragic plot is overwhelmingly the thing that counts. We can see him putting himself on guard early about the poetry of poetic drama when the drama is tragic. Before he goes into tragedy, when he is only pointing out our natural pleasure in imitations, he is careful to remark that sometimes this pleasure is taken chiefly in admiring the technical achievement of the imitator, so that we may even enjoy the picture of a corpse if it is done skillfully. We would remark that there may be pleasure in it, but there is also a good deal of pain; which is precisely what Aristotle is compelled presently to emphasize. The plot of a tragedy, he says flatly, and repeats many times, must be such as to cause us plain pity and terror; these are unpleasant emotions. Pity is a wretched business, which not only distracts us from our duties of the moment but incapacitates us, by destroying our animal faith in the goodness of the natural world; and terror is disordering and needs no comment. He would have the playwright steel himself constantly to his endeavor, never relaxing his severity and feeding us with a turn of action which would mitigate these emotions. It is my impression that the gentle and idealizing critics do not fancy Aristotle's toughness about this, but then it is hard to believe that they have assimilated the horror of the actual tragedies that he is reporting. It was sheer good luck, says Aristotle, that the Attic playwrights found a grand source for their tragic plots, as if made to order for them, in the stock of common legends about the ancient royal houses. The legends are improbable, and for tragic purposes almost too good to be true, but they were well known, and could be repeated as if they were true. The great families of the legends would seem to have been highly specialized in domestic horrors.

> Let us see, then [says Aristotle], what kinds of incident strike us as horrible or piteous. In a deed of this sort the parties must necessarily be either friends, or enemies, or indifferent to one another. Now when enemy does it on enemy, there is nothing to move us to pity either in his doing or in his meditating the deed, except so far as the actual pain of the sufferer is concerned; and the same is true when the parties are indifferent to one another. Whenever the tragic deed, however, is done within the family — when murder or the like is done or meditated by brother on brother, by son on father, by mother on son, or son on mother —

these are the situations the poet should seek after. The traditional stories, accordingly, must be kept as they are, e. g., the murder of Clytaemnestra by Orestes and of Eriphyle by Alcmaeon.[1]

It is grim. Yet these murderers must be represented as good men, indeed a little better than ourselves, not so much depraved as given to errors of judgment, or we should not identify ourselves with them by sympathetic imagination, and must fail to experience the pity.

It is clear that our absorption in such tragedies indicates a behavior of the second sort that we noted just now; they are not so much for the trifling intrinsic pleasure which comes from the steady flow of the poetic diction, but for the sake of the eventual happiness to which they are the means. Tragedy for tragedy's sake is hardly the name of a rational motivation, and if there is such a thing we call it masochistic and destructive. Aristotle's position is a good functional or even Darwinian one. And the function that he specifies is *katharsis*: the purgation of all the pity and fear from the psyche through the technique of tapping them by means of the horrors of the play. That will be a healthy relief when it comes, and most certainly a pleasant one.

He repeats this formulation a good deal too, like a paradigm that the teacher writes upon the blackboard. With what oral elaboration in this instance we do not know, but none

---

[1] The translation is Bywater's, in Principal W. Hamilton Fyfe's *Aristotle's Art of Poetry* (Oxford).

is incorporated in the written text for us now. *Katharsis* is
a gross physiological metaphor out of *materia medica*,
whereby the draining of the poisonous slops from the body
is made to stand for the subtle psychic relief under the
fourth figure of metaphorical substitution, which proceeds
by analogy; this would be according to Aristotle. He does
not miss in his linguistic analysis, but he is not so proficient
in the psychic mysteries. If he is sometimes a pre-Darwinian naturalist, he makes it all too clear that psychologically,
for all his shrewdness, he dwells in an untechnical pre-
Freudian night. For my part, I cannot help but find this
figure of purgation inept; it is too hard to apply it and see
how the clearing out of the painful emotions must follow
from artificially prompting them; there must be subtler
mechanisms at work. Yet who will disagree with him, once
the point is made, and deny that somehow composure is restored to the auditors of proper drama, and even to its readers? And what an excellent thing that must be! A recent work
is entitled *The Age of Anxiety*. But history repeats itself,
and it must have been Aristotle's notion that his was that
age. Pity for misfortune greater than the victim has deserved,
at a time when such misfortune is endemic in our community,
and terror because it happens to people as good as we are —
these emotions are vicious company for the vital and constructive thoughts in our heads. They sap our courage, they
paralyze our initiative, while actual defeat and frustration
are brought only the nearer by our inaction. And living in

apprehension, we will try anything that promises to restore the equable temper which conditions a good vital effort.

We must think of Aristotle as a true humanist, a Greek very close to his national culture and beyond Plato in his responsiveness, as having the noble and improbable insight that the tragic art purges men of their fears and makes them better men. But to grasp the technique of this purging we have to make a configuration of our own, and go beyond Aristotle. I think the trick to try will be something like this: to see if the lavish, the all-but-incessant poetry with which the Greek dramatists invest their tragedy does not throw a decent obscurity over the terrible events; and though of course it does not promise to avert these, if at least it does not immunize us against their terror. Incidentally, such a strategy would be most agreeable to the careful critical sense, in that it would bring the tragic plot and the poetic diction back into reciprocal working relation, and not leave them separated and at cross-purposes as Aristotle does. Now the terror we feel is not wholly stupid, it is not born of total blindness, for our eyes may be fastened precisely upon the shapes of doom. But that is all we shall see if we are terrified, it is all we can think about, and we freeze from staring at the Gorgon's head. So at the lowest estimate it may be by a mere technique of diversion from the obsessive horror that we are restored to sanity. To recover presence of mind is to make the mind resume its most gallant and extravagant activities, and so to put off again the season when it must revert, if it ever reverts, to a primitive monomania under the pain. All this will seem indirect, and casuistical; but in these days we do not discount the psyche's capacity for improvisation.

According to Aristotle, a logical intellect must preside over the manipulation of the tragic plot. At any rate that is what we conclude from his emphasis upon the probability of the events, and the suitable and common types of character in the *dramatis personae* who enact them. He says the plot deals with universals rather than particulars. The poetic diction in the meantime is imitating busily, that is to say, it is going away from the universals of the plot a thousand times to evoke its particulars. And so we have an anticipation of that very opposition of reason and sensibility which characterizes the world of art and beauty for Immanuel Kant, in that modern work which is regarded as the foundation of systematic aesthetics. But in Aristotle the two components do not work together, and the human drama of their opposition is not made clear.

We are later than Aristotle culturally and, as it would follow, philosophically. Aesthetic historians, severally, tell us why the *Critique of Judgment* could not have appeared before its actual date of 1790. A grossly simplified and lay version of this why would be as follows.

The Greek philosophers, our ancestors, were motivated by a pride of intellect, and a contempt for free sensibility. The Eleatics gave the cue when they renounced the sensible world, at least up to the limits of human strength, and occupied themselves in the contemplation of pure determinate being. And presently there is a theology which sets up a "divine" world of pure being as actual, though invisible, and allows the human soul, as a rational being divinely implanted in the natural body, partly to inhabit it. This dogma was in the grand style, and formed a great stream of the European tradition, and its force is not spent yet. Plato, however, had too much resourcefulness, and healthy worldly interest, to stop long in the arid otherworld of pure intellection. The Platonic Idea is his invention. The rational principle comes down to earth; it grips the matter of common nature and transforms it into what is orderly and rational yet still existent, till this existential world itself partakes of the nature of the divine world. Naturally, the Ideas must take on more and more complexity if they want to grip the natural objects in the whole manifold of their concretions; naturally, Plato did not go a great way in developing them. But we will make a long jump and come to his successor Hegel, who extends the range of the Ideas brilliantly, and with so much success that he is able to talk of the Concrete Universal. And what is that? The Concrete Universal is the common or abstract universal, the bare concept, prodigiously improved internally; so elaborated and organized that now it hopes to take into its grip *all* the qualities that sensibility discovers in the concretions of nature; till reason and sensibility shall have identical objects, and logic and aesthetics become one. But Hegel's success with this project was specious; the analytical intelligence of the last century has been in painful revolt against it, and the latest revolt is that harsh and tormented movement, the current "existentialism."

If Hegel is Plato's pious and dutiful successor, his unwitting successors have been legion. They are the men who have seen what intellect was really good for, and made it pay; men of the last three or four centuries, whose intellectual formations have been close, persistent, and specialized, aggregating into what we call our modern science; they produced the industrial revolution. By the time of Kant, but scarcely before then, it was possible to say a very simple thing about the faculty of specialized reason, or intellect, for it had been empirically established. Thus: it is the instrument of our appetitive life. Kant made the identification clearly, though he did not surrender all the aspirations he entertained on behalf of reason; Schopenhauer and Bergson repeated it with the indignation of disillusioned men; and it is Freud's basic assumption that reason is the technical organ by which the human creature reacts to environment and secures his desires. The Concrete Universal or Idea did not have the comprehensive grip it tried for, and the intellectualists have reverted to the abstract or common universal. The latter's grip is very effective indeed for its own purposes, but these do not include anything like a comprehension of nature; and nature is still as "infinite" or boundless as the ancients hatefully called it, inviolable in its contingency and plenitude.

Not for one minute is this reporter tempted by ambition, neither is he inclined by temperament, to "reject" the scientific achievement. He understands that reason is the differentia of our species, the organ which raises it above the others in effectiveness, gives it the dominion over nature which was promised in our story of creation. We have used it well, to obtain more and better goods from nature. We are still, or rather we are again, a consciously animal species, for which the appetitive life has every priority, being the condition prior to all those aspirations which are not appetitive, if there are such aspirations. But just now the predicament of high-minded persons is slightly embarrassing. A human aspiration is probably the strangest and most characteristic of the human behaviors, since it is a move away from the line of the common economy, and covets what would not seem quite possible, a reckless and pointed suspension of animal interest. It is evidently a *proprium* of the species, if not the essential *differentia*. The form that aspiration once liked to take was intellectual, as with Plato. But at the moment this is not so good, now that intellectual attainment is scarcely the rarity it once seemed to be, and now that it is so firmly identified with common animal motivation.

I imagine that the general topic of this Symposium, upon which we concentrate soberly for three full days, tempts us all into magnificent secret strategies. Perhaps, for example, we find ourselves supposing that our aspiration, the thing which will best certify our humanism by essaying what is slightly superhuman, is now going to be under the aesthetic form. I believe this will require of us behaviors that are not for the sake of dominion over nature, of which the technical organ is reason, but for the sake of something as impractical as gentleness, or love, whose organ is sensibility. It is difficult to describe it behavioristically. What we love we can look at, we can crave the presence of, or if we are absented we can "imitate" in the way of imagination and art, we can explore continually for fresh insights — but what can we really, adequately do? There is singularly little in the way of overt action that we can do to express the diffuse and massive excitement that comes over us from love. The term, of course, will refer to Agape rather than Eros. In its full range it will not mean simply our love for our own kind, as in happy families, though that is an admirable attainment, but what is still more quixotic, the love of nature. This last extension is not necessary for the ethical aspiration. But it is necessary for religion, if nature means "everything in the world," and it is necessary for art; in these aspirations the achievement is finer than ethical, though not more heroic.

The easiest perspective upon such aspirations comes from the naturalistic description. The creature was formed within nature, but immediately nature became his environment, external to him; whereupon self-preservation depended upon enforcing his needs and uses against environment. A risk is run in the formation of any organic species, lest it

fail to establish its vital economy firmly against an environment horribly unresponsive to the creature's poor techniques. But suppose he is man, the technologist himself,
and does establish his economy, and comes to feel secure in
it, well assured that the environment will yield him its favors
when he demands them, and that its bounty is not going to
be exhausted — what then? It is my impression that the
complete naturalist, with whatever reservations when it
comes to interpreting it, must attest the next thing as follows.
The creature begins to devote some of his leisure and unex-
pended energy — his technique has earned them — to re-
versing the normal attitude to environment, so that where
there was only dominion and use there develops a sentimental fixation upon certain natural objects, which is conspicuously disproportionate to their utility. These become
his "precious objects," the objects which he prizes at more
than their utility value, for he loves them. In this role, as we
have seen, he is capable of only redundant and nondescript
behaviors. There is little he can do for the object, which,
after all, is an alien and inviolable natural object; nor is
there anything he can do for himself, since fixation started
where the utility of the object left off; so that it is no wonder
that his sentimental exhibitions in the eyes of a sardonic
naturalist may seem slightly absurd. But presently, as if
because he is tired of repeating the same little endearments,
yet is still under the compulsion of his tender feelings, while
he cannot invent actions forceful enough or various enough

to express them, the sentimentalist employs his wits and transforms himself into the man of sensibility; and now he has infinite resources. Poetry lies before him, and the future of poetry is immense. Now the whole of nature, rather than its obvious and familiar concretions, becomes the object of his affection, so that he will be ready to stop wherever he may be traversing it, and make observations and imitations *en passant*; for there is nature always and everywhere. He is on the watch for natural effects which are not useful but brilliant and vivid, i.e. notable, as for a man carrying a notebook. With experience his perceptions become constantly more acute, and they improve still further as he becomes proficient linguistically, i.e. in the language, or medium, of imitation.

This is the crude sketch of a natural history of sentiment and sensibility, and of the arts which exist for their most perfect expression. It might easily prompt the satirical treatment if it tells the truth, and does not disguise the illogic, and a certain promiscuity, which obtain in these formations. It deals with an odd sort of behavior; but there is so much of it that the naturalist may be led to take it professionally, that is to say seriously. He would have to speculate upon the function of a gratuitous behavior; the economy of an attitude which seems determined to be out of economic character. Its real motivation will have to be an unconscious one.

As speculations go, this one is probably not too hard. If the creature's natural adaptations are successful, then the awk-

ward honors that are being paid to nature have a festal
character, and festivals look quite serious, lending themselves as they do to the greatest public occasions. With respect to the given adaptation to which the festival logically
refers, we should expect that the festal effect must be strongly
confirmatory, or conservative; it would confirm the adaptation which has succeeded, whose success is the occasion and
public content of the festive art; and surely a good adaptation is entitled to some confirmation. The arts will scarcely
know that they exert a conservative influence, though this
has often been said about religion; it is the naturalist who
would know it; he might think it important. Furthermore, or
perhaps this is a corollary principle, the arts will induce the
sense of security, and they will be tonic for the apprehensive
or timid. Here we have worked back to the old topic of the
*Poetics*. But now we are dealing with successes, not tragedies, and the fearful do not exactly pass their nights in wake-
fulness and trembling when the times are easy and the feeling about things is a feeling of success. Let us say at the least
that the temperamentally fearful obtain through art a proper
confidence. What they think they do is to attach themselves
in joy, and perhaps with a mystic sense of communion, to
the alien form of nature, and it is as if they had never a care
of their own in the world; but there is more than coincidence
in the fact that they have negotiated successfully with nature
for their needs. Joy in beauty is wonderfully spontaneous,
and it is impossible for us ever to feel more innocent or, as

aestheticians put it, "disinterested." Many critics of art are willing to stop uncritically upon that note, and it does well enough for them if they are not Aristotle. It is the duty of the naturalist to look a little further. According to my own guess, he will conclude that a certain exhilaration or exuberance of spirit has been achieved, such as must rest probably upon a sturdy foundation of animal faith, and is, considering the peril of the animal predicament in the world, propitious.

In art we are conditioned through the spectacle of success to the habit of sensibility, and among other services it will serve us in the evil hour. The tragic drama, devoted to unsuccess, shows the way. So we come back finally to our starting point. The tragic Greek plots that Aristotle studied move at nearly all times with a great train of free and energetic imagery, and to the handsomest phonetic or musical accompaniment. These are the forms of the sensibility that the heroes use in actual speech when they fall upon adversities. With my small Greek I seem at least here and there to verify these effects, to which scholars have testified. To an audience which was as Greek as the play itself, the plight of the heroes, though mortal, was not too terrible, since the heroes themselves were not terrified out of their wits but continued in easy exercise of the most liberal powers of mind; and by sympathy the auditors became for the time being as the heroes. As public affairs the tragedies, of course, were exemplary and normative; the spectators were a little more enabled to go through with their own vile occasions.

Tragedy is the literary form where the strength of sensibility is really tested. It is a great *tour de force* in art, the work of the virtuoso. The heroes fail of success, and know they are failing. No practical adaptation is possible, and the animal struggle ceases, though not for the reason that it ceases in the arts of success. But sensibility operates all the same; the focus of dramatic interest is turned altogether upon sensibility; the issue is known, and the plot is not the thing now, the heroic style is the thing. We are reminded of the situation of the religious man when he says: "Though he slay me, yet will I trust him." This religious man must have had a long conditioning. We may be sure that his aspiration did not begin with so immoderate a leap of animal faith, but started modestly in the flush of his early experiences of God's goodness; these repeated themselves, till they confirmed his courage and formed his religious character; this now is irreversible, and the time is past when he could denounce God and die in stony hatred or in terror.

In conclusion I will quote from the talk in a scene where a famous hero dies. But perhaps no one of us now has the ear to follow those remarkable Greek meters sensitively, certainly not I; while it would only defame the masterpieces to read from our miserable English translations. In the spirit of Aristotle I resort to that fourth figure of metaphor which is the substitution by analogy. It will be Shakespeare's scene where Antony dies. There are differences between the classi-

cal and the Shakespearian, but perhaps they are outweighed
by the analogies.

Antony's war against Caesar has come to grief, and if he
does not wish to be taken captive it is time for him to die.
He appeals to his servant Eros, who is pledged to kill him
when the moment comes:

> *Thou art sworn, Eros,*
> *That when the exigent should come — which now*
> *Is come indeed — when I should see behind me*
> *The inevitable prosecution of*
> *Disgrace and horror, that, on my command,*
> *Then thou would'st kill me. Do't; the time is come.*
> *Thou strik'st not me, 'tis Caesar thou defeat'st.*
> *Put color in thy cheek.*

Antony's rich poetic vein does not show diminution. The
verse flows easily from it, not muddied or thickened by
emotion. But Eros will not strike, and Antony must argue
with him:

> *Eros,*
> *Would'st thou be window'd in great Rome and see*
> *Thy master thus with pleach'd arms, bending down*
> *His corrigible neck, his face subdued*
> *To penetrative shame, whilst the wheel'd seat*
> *Of fortunate Caesar, drawn before him, branded*
> *His baseness that ensued?*

A reader is obliged to suppose that Antony folds his arms
as he speaks, and bends his neck, to suit the words; his lively
imitation tries two media at once, for the benefit of an

auditor who is not only stubborn but a little bit unimagina-
tive. The poetry is of the highest inventiveness, and of a
veteran sensibility.

We stop here. Though there are several ingenious and
beautiful turns to come before Antony actually dies, I
assume that the point has been made. Antony is purged of
terror by his own poetry, and we are purged. Even Cleopatra
will show that she has been affected by his example, when
she invites her own death in these words:

> *We'll bury him; and then, what's brave, what's noble,*
> *Let's do it after the high Roman fashion,*
> *And make death proud to take us.*

But we must quarrel a little with her aesthetics, which does
not exactly take into account the technical *katharsis*. She did
not hear the speeches I have quoted, and seems to think that
Antony merely fell upon his sword like any simple Roman
soldier. It would have been excellent for Antony to be an
antique Roman, and a Stoic. It would have taught him to die
decently, if that means to die dumbly, in a constriction of
sensibility, as by a feat of virtual anaesthesia; for that is
possible too. But that is not the line of the tragic hero. It is
better for him to finish when he is in full character, when
the world is beautiful to his sensibility. He is then perfect
in his fidelity to the human career, and ought to be approved
by the naturalist as he is loved by the aspiring spectator.

*Allen Tate*

# LONGINUS

*Allen Tate*

# LONGINUS

To BEGIN an essay with a silent apology to the subject is
commendable, but one should not expect the reader to
be interested in it. I allude to the ignorance in which I had
underestimated Longinus, before I reread him after twenty
years, because I am convinced that it is typical. Who reads
Longinus? I do not mean to say literally that he is not read.
There is an excellent recent study by Mr. Elder Olson;
there are the fine books by Mr. T. R. Henn and Mr. Samuel
H. Monk,[1] which persons of the critical interest should
know something about and doubtless do. Until these books
appeared, there had been no serious consideration of
Longinus since Saintsbury's *A History of Criticism* (1900).
In some twenty-five years of looking at criticism in the
United States and England, I have not seen, with the exceptions already noticed, a reference to the περὶ ὕψους which
is of more than historical interest. One might, with misplaced
antiquarian zeal, find the name, if not much more, of Aris-

[1] *Longinus and English Criticism*, by T. R. Henn (Cambridge, 1934); and
*The Sublime: A Study of Critical Theories in XVIII-Century England*, by
Samuel H. Monk (New York, 1935).

totle in the pages of a fashionable journal like *Horizon*; one would have to go to the learned journals, which few critics see, to find even the name of Longinus. Until Mr. Henn and Mr. Monk reminded us of him, he had been dropped out of active criticism since the end of the eighteenth century. I should like to believe that these excellent scholars have brought about a Longinian revival. Mr. Herbert Read informs me that Coleridge in *Table Talk* spoke of him as "no very profound critic." It must seem to us today that Coleridge buried him in that remark. I am not confident that I shall succeed where Mr. Monk and Mr. Henn failed (if they did fail), that what I am about to say will exhume Longinus.

## I

This is not the occasion to establish a correct English title for περὶ ὕψους. (In the New Testament ὕψος means not the physical heavens [οὐρανός] but something like "on high.") To my mind, the idea of height or elevation contained in the title, *Of the Height of Eloquence,* which was given to the work by the first English translator, John Hall, in 1652, is more exact than *On the Sublime,* which carries with it the accretions of Boileau and the English eighteenth century, and the different meanings contributed later by Burke and Kant, which are far removed from anything that I have been able to find in this third- (or is it first- ?) century treatise. So far from Kant's is Longinus' conception of "sublimity" that one pauses at the marvelous semantic history of the term. In Chapter IX Longinus quotes a passage from the *Iliad,* Book XX, about the war of the gods, and comments: "Yet these things terrible as they are, if they are not taken as an allegory are altogether blasphemous and destructive of what is seemly." To allegorize infinite magnitude, quantity beyond the range of the eye, is to reduce it to the scale of what Kant called the Beautiful as distinguished from the Sublime. The "sublimity" of the passage, in the Kantian sense, Longinus could not accept. These shifts of meaning are beyond the scope of my interest and my competence. Three other brief and confusing parallels will fix in our minds the difficulties of Longinus' title. His insight, perhaps unique in antiquity, which is contained in the distinction between the "persuasion" of oratory and the "transport" of what, for want of a better phrase, one may call the literary effect, reappears in this century as neo-symbolism and surrealism. Some twenty years ago the Abbé Bremond decided that "transport" meant religious mysticism, and wrote a book called *la Poésie pure.* In England, about thirty years ago, Arthur Machen, of whom few people of the generations younger than mine have heard, the author of *The Hill of Dreams* and other novels after Huysmans, wrote a small critical book called *Hieroglyphics.* Machen proposed to discern the real thing in literature with a test that he called "ecstasy," but what made Machen ecstatic left many persons cold. At any rate, the Greek word in Longinus that we trans-

late as "transport" is ἔκστασις. Had Boileau not stuffed
Longinus with neo-classical "authority," would he have been
discovered by the French and English romantics, to whom
he could have spoken from another if equally wrong direction? This topic may be dropped with the observation that
literary history is no more orderly than any other history.

I shall, then, in the following remarks, think of the two
key terms in Longinus, ὕψος and ἔκστασις, as respectively
Elevation of Language and Transport; but I cannot expect
to disentangle them from each other. They contain, in their
interrelations, a version of a persistent ambiguity of critical
reference which appeared with Aristotle, had vigorous life
up to Coleridge (with whom it comes back disguised), and
now eggs on the edifying controversy of the contemporary
English and American critics: Ransom, Cleanth Brooks,
Read, Leavis, Richards, Blackmur, and Winters. Is Elevation an objective quality of the literary work? Is Transport
its subjective reference denoting the emotions of the reader
— or the "hearer," as Longinus calls him — as he receives
the impact of Elevation? Does either term, Elevation or
Transport, point to anything sufficiently objective to be isolated for critical discussion?

This is not the moment to answer that question, if I were
competent to answer it. Our first duty is to find out how
Longinus asks it. After defining Elevation tautologically, in
Chapter I, as "a kind of supreme excellence of discourse"
(ἐξοχή τις λόγων ἐστὶ τὰ ὕψη), he describes its effect:

*For what is out of the common* affects the hearer not
to persuade but to entrance (οὐ γὰρ εἰς πειθὼ τοὺς
ἀκροωμένους ἀλλ' εἰς ἔκστασιν ἄγει τὰ ὑπερφυᾶ).
It moves to wonder and surprise, and always wins
against what is merely delightful or persuasive. It is
not enough in one or two passages of a work to exhibit
invention schooled by experience, nor again the fine
order and distribution of its parts, nor even these qualities displayed throughout. Rather, I suggest, does the
sublime, fitly expressed, pierce everything like a flash
of lightning. . . .[2]

*Not to persuade, but to entrance, like a flash of lightning.*
In these words Longinus breaks with the rhetoricians who
had dominated ancient criticism since Aristotle, four to six
hundred years before him, and who continued to dominate
it until the seventeenth century. Neither Longinus nor Dante,
on *De Vulgari Eloquentia,* had any influence on critical
theory after them, until the time of Boileau, when Longinus
was used to justify rules that he had never made; Dante's
criticism has languished in the department of biography;
at best, in the history of criticism, as a document of the time.

[2] With the exception of a few phrases I quote throughout from the translation by Frank Granger (London, 1935), which seems to me the most per-
spicuous English version. The exceptions are the result of a collation of
the Granger and other versions with what is probably the definitive scholarly translation, by W. Rhys Roberts (Cambridge, 1899). All the modern
translations render ὕψος as "sublime," and it has obviously been necessary
to keep the word when it occurs in a quoted passage.

## II

Chapter II opens with the question: "We must first discuss whether there is an art of the sublime." In the Greek, the phrase is ὕψους τις ἢ βάθους τέχνη — "an art of height or of depth"; but the word we should attend is τέχνη, "art," which the Greeks used for any teachable skill, from metal-working to music and medicine. They applied the term to all the skills of making for which an objective rationale could be devised. Longinus explains the views of Caecilius, the opponent of uncertain identity whom the περὶ ὕψους was written to refute, who believed that elevation of language came through nature alone, that the great writer, born great, needs nothing but his birth. In this controversy of lively acrimony with a man who may have been dead three hundred years (such was the leisure of antiquity), Longinus at the beginning of his essay opposes, in opposing Caecilius, both the Platonic and the Aristotelian doctrines, and holds that style is a compound of natural talent and conscious method. He thus parts with Plato's "divine madness" in the *Ion*, and implicitly claims for Thought and Diction, two of the nonstructural elements in Aristotle's analysis of tragedy, a degree of objectivity that Aristotle's rhetorical view of poetic language could not include.

If literary method cannot alone produce a style, the judgment of which, says Longinus, "is the last fruit of long experience," it can "help us to speak at the right length

and to the occasion." How much interpretation of a casual
observation such as this, which is only common sense, the
modern scholiast is entitled to develop, I do not know. Although Longinus may have in mind merely the orator and
the *public* occasion, may we just see him reaching out for a
criterion of objectivity for any sort of literary composition?
The "right length" is the adaptation of form to subject; and
is not the "occasion" the relation between the poet and the
person to whom the poem is addressed? We have, fore-
shadowed here, I think, a principle of dramatic propriety,
a sense of the "point of view" in composition, the prime
literary strategy which can never be made prescriptive, but
which exhibits its necessity equally in its operation and in
its lapse. Later, discussing meter, Longinus tells us that
Elevation cannot be achieved in the trochaic, or tripping,
meter, and we may dismiss the remark as the perennial
fallacy which identifies certain fixed effects with certain
meters. But if we can imagine "Lycidas" written in trochees
and "The Raven" in iambuses, we might suppose the one
would be worse, the other considerably better. And if we
look at "length" and "occasion" in somewhat different
terms, we shall find ourselves again in the thick of one of
our own controversies. Does not the occasion force upon the
poet the objective and communicable features of his work?
Are they not Mr. Winters' theory of the relation of "feeling"
to "rational content" and Mr. Ransom's theory of a "texture" within a "structure"?

In exceeding the literal text of Longinus in this matter, I hope that I have not also stretched two living critics into an agreement which they have scarcely acknowledged; nor should I ask them to acknowledge Longinus as their fore-runner. I suggest that Longinus' question "Is there an art of Elevation?" is the question we are asking today, somewhat as follows: can there be a criticism of convincing objectivity which approaches the literary work through the analysis of style and which arrives at its larger aspects through that aperture?

That is the question of our time. In asking it, are we not following Longinus rather than Aristotle? Aristotle began with the conspicuous "larger aspects" of a mature literary genre, Greek tragedy, and got around to the problems of poetic language only at the end, and as a rhetorician (except for one curious remark about metaphor) who offers us shrewd but merely schematic advice about the use of figures.

### III

If there is an art of Elevation, if there is possible a coherent criticism of literature through its language, it follows that we must examine good and bad writers together, in order to arrive, not at rules, but at that "judgment of style which is the fruit of long experience"; to arrive at that sense of the length and the occasion which will permit us, as poets, to imitate not Homer's style but its excellence, in our own language. It is here that intensive literary criticism and

literary tradition work together; it is here that we arrive at
the idea of a literary tradition which does not enjoin the
slavery of repetition, but of the emulation which comes of
insight. We shall have of course to deal as best we can with
the ambiguity of Longinus' word τέχνη. By the "art of
height or of depth" does he mean criticism? Or does he
mean the "art" of the poet? He means, I take it, both; and
it is proper that he should. For our sense of the achievement
of the past may issue in a critical acquisition of knowledge
which is not to be put away in the attic when the creative
moment comes. At this point one may profitably notice two
characteristic defects, defects of its quality, that proud and
self-sufficient writers fall into in attempting the elevated
style. "Frigidity," says Longinus, is the overelaboration of
the academic writer, a violation of length due to aiming at
"the curious and the artificial." The "feeling" (or the detail) is unreal in the sense that it is on a scale smaller than its
intelligible form. Likewise, the opposite fault — and in
describing it Longinus has written as good criticism as any
I know — of Thomas Wolfe and the contemporary lyrical
novel; he says:

> Theodorus calls it the mock-inspired. It is emotion out
> of place and empty where there is no need of it, or lack
> of proportion where proportion is needed. Some writ-
> ers fall into a maudlin mood and digress from their
> subject into their own tedious emotion. Thus they
> show bad form and leave their audience unimpressed:

necessarily, for they are in a state of rapture, and the audience is not.

If this is the performance of the writer great by nature and beyond "art," Henry James gives us his dreary portrait: "The writer who cultivates his instinct rather than his awareness sits by finally in a stale and shrinking puddle." His awareness of what? I should say of the "occasion" and the "length," the sense of limiting structure and of what, within that limit, is to be objectively communicated and made known. This sense becomes operative through "art," τέχνη, technique, the controlled awareness *through* language of what can be made actual *in* language, resulting in a just, if unpredictable, proportion between what Longinus calls the "emotion" and the "subject." Doubtless, any experienced reader of literature can point to the failures of great writers in the two extremes of disproportion corresponding to two forms of pride that prevent the complete discovery of the subject: the pride of intellect and the pride of feeling, the pride of will and the pride of instinct. (Perhaps the history of the imagination is the pendulum between these extremes.) Mr. Blackmur has shown us in the past few years how the thesis in Dostoevsky distorts or even wrecks the theme, the imaginative actuality in which the form ought to have been discovered under pressure of its internal necessity. In a more recent writer, D. H. Lawrence, we get both extremes of pride: the attack on the intellect in behalf of instinct, instinct itself hardening into a core of abstraction which operates as intellectual pride, as thesis; not as realized form.

The instances of "disproportion" could be multiplied, but I pause to remark my own disgression, and to ask, as the eighteenth-century critics seem not to have done, whether there is not already, in what I have said, a certain excess of gloss, commentary cut loose from the text commented upon, a self-indulgence which seems to attribute to the subject a comprehension which one is covertly claiming for oneself? Criticism should no doubt observe the same proprieties of occasion and length that we require of the imagination; but it has seldom done so, and I think with good reason. If criticism is only secondary to literature, it is thus the dependent partner, and for the hazards that it must face in every generation it must constantly worry the past for support, and make too much of what it revives, or perhaps even make it into something different. Perhaps I have got out of the περὶ ὕψους at this stage of the discussion only a general insight available, if not always used, as common property since Coleridge. Yet we should remember that Longinus alone seems to have achieved it in the ancient world.

I have been trying to see the outlines, before I move on to some of the particular judgments in the περὶ ὕψους, of a possible framework into which to put Longinus' profound but topical dialectic. In the same chapter (II) in which the proportions of length and occasion are held to be established through "art" or method, he writes this crucial passage:

Demosthenes says somewhere that in ordinary life

luck is the greatest good, and that it cannot exist without another which is not inferior to it, namely prudent conduct. Following him, we might say, in the case of style, that nature takes the place of good luck; and art, of prudent conduct. *Most important of all, we must learn from art the fact that some elements of style depend upon nature alone.*

At this point four pages of the manuscript disappear, a loss of the first importance to critical theory. If the amateur Hellenist reads from classical criticism a passage in which the word "nature" occurs, he is likely to read it with Boileau or the English eighteenth century, and get entangled in the thickets of "nature," which they opposed to "art," when they were not effecting a compromise by making art nature to advantage dressed; and so on. It seems to me that we ought to support the passage just quoted with a full sense of the special kind of judgment that Longinus brings to bear upon the actual texture of Greek literature; he produces many examples which cannot be cited here. We could then just see in it the first declaration of independence from the practical, forensic eloquence of the rhetoricians.

"Most important of all, we must learn from art the fact that some elements of style depend upon nature alone." In trying to understand this nice oxymoron, I shall take risks which are perhaps not greater than those taken by most commentators on the *Poetics*. Most important of all, I make Longinus say, we learn from the development of technique that stylistic autonomy is a delusion, because style comes into existence only as it discovers the subject; and conversely the subject exists only after it is formed by the style. No literary work is perfect, no subject perfectly formed. Style reveals that which is not style in the process of forming it. Style does not create the subject, it discovers it. The fusion of art and nature, of technique and subject, can never exceed the approximate; the margin of imperfection, of the un-formed, is always there — nature intractable to art, art unequal to nature. The converse of Longinus' aphorism will further elucidate it: we must learn from nature that some elements of subject matter, in a literary work, "depend" upon art alone. There is a reciprocal relation, not an identity — not, certainly, the identity of form and content — a dynamic, shifting relation between technique and subject; and they reveal each other. This is my sense of Longinus' primary insight. It is an insight of considerable subtlety that has a special claim to the attention of our generation.

## IV

I suppose we should agree that by and large the critical method of the *Poetics* is inductive. Aristotle's generalizations proceed from a scrutiny of one kind of literature, drama, chiefly from one kind of drama, tragedy, and from one kind of tragedy, Greek. Longinus repeats Aristotle's animadversions on "character," which Aristotle seems to think need not be much developed if the "plot" is good. We must constantly remind ourselves of the narrow range of literature at the command of the two great critics of antiquity; they lacked the novel, for one thing, and Aristotle evidently did not consider the works of his great predecessor and teacher worthy of the name of "poetry." The larger conception of a literature does not appear in the *Poetics*. Although Longinus, trained as he must have been in the rhetorical schools, did not see clearly whither he was heading, it is just the awareness of *literature at large* which raises his theory of the relation of language and subject to a higher degree of useful generality than any literary theory before him had reached. He is the first, though necessarily incomplete, literary critic. His question, put again, in its wider implications, is: what distinguishes literature from practical oratory, from history? A quality, he says in effect, beyond an immediate purpose. His discussion of imagination is what we should expect: it is the classical rhetorician's view of the image as a "mental picture," which he, along with his age, seems to believe must be laid on the work discreetly from the top. Yet the distinction between two widely different purposes in the controlled use of language puts his doctrine on a high yet accessible level of empirical generalization, and makes it possible for him to look beyond specific conventions to estimate the value of a literature offering a great variety of forms and structures.

It has been supposed by many critics that Longinus is not interested in structure, that his doctrine of "transport" and the "lightning flash" anticipates the romantic *frisson*, or that Pope did it justice when he called in Longinus to help him "snatch a grace beyond the reach of art." I think I have shown that Longinus would reject that art which is beyond its own reach. And what, in fact, I now wish to show is that Longinus is quite prepared to put his finger directly upon the problem of structure, and by implication to tell us that structure is not in the formal "type" or genre, a viable body of special conventions, such as the lyric, the ode, or the epic provides, but exists in the language of the poem.

After discussing, in Chapters VIII and IX, the five sources of Elevation in language (to which I shall return), he analyzes the effect, in terms of structure, of Sappho's Ode to Anactoria, beginning: φαίνεταί μοι κῆνος ἴσος θεοῖσιν. The analysis is brief (everything in Longinus is brief but the lacunae in the text), yet it is probably the first example in criticism of structural analysis of a lyric poem. (I ought for my purpose here to know more than I do, which is virtually nothing, about the ancient theory of the Passions.) I quote the entire passage:

> Let us now go on to see whether we have anything further by means of which we can raise our words to the sublime. Since, then, in the substance of everything, we find certain elements which naturally belong to it, we should of course find one cause of the sublime by always choosing the most relevant circumstances and by compounding them (ἐπισυνθέσει) to make, so

to speak, one body (ἕν τι σῶμα ποιεῖν). For the audience is attracted, first by our choice of topics (ὁ μὲν γὰρ τῇ ἐκλογῇ . . . . τῶν λημμάτων), and second, by the conciseness of our exposition. For example, Sappho takes from their actual setting the feelings that accompany the frenzy of love. Where then does she display her skill? In the tact with which she chooses and binds together supreme and intense feelings.

> *Peer of Gods he seemeth to me, the blissful*
> *Man who sits and gazes at thee before him,*
> *Close beside thee sits, and in silence hears thee*
>   *Silverly speaking,*
>
> *Laughing love's low laughter. Oh this, this only*
> *Stirs the troubled heart in my breast to tremble!*
> *For should I but see thee a little moment,*
>   *Straight is my voice hushed;*
>
> *Yea, my tongue is broken, and through and*
>   *through me*
> *'Neath the flesh impalpable fire runs tingling;*
> *Nothing see mine eyes, and a noise of roaring*
>   *Waves in my ear sounds;*
>
> *Sweat runs down in rivers, a tremor seizes*
> *All my limbs, and paler than grass in autumn,*
> *Caught by pains of menacing death, I falter,*
>   *Lost in the love trance. . . .*

Do you not wonder how she gives chase at once to soul and body, to words and tongue, to sight and color,

all as if scattered abroad, how *uniting contradictions*,[3]
she is frozen and burns, she raves and is wise? For
either she is panic-stricken or at point of death; she is
haunted not by a single emotion but their *whole company*.[4]

Towards the end of the περὶ ὕψους there is some scattered
commentary on the rhetorical figures; but in the criticism of
Sappho the language is not that of the tropes and figures. In
so far as it concerns emotion, it is "psychological," if not
very exact, even in the terms of the classical psychology of
the passions; yet perhaps it is not too much to claim for
Longinus' perception of opposites in this poem, of the positive compulsion given tension by its negative, that it goes
deeper and is more attentive to what the poem says than
anything that Arnold has to say about Keats' or Milton's
poetry. *He is trying to see what is happening in the poem.*
If he is hampered by his affective terms, so was Mr. T. S.
Eliot when, in an early essay, he was getting at a similar
play of opposites (what Mr. Cleanth Brooks has since called
"paradox") by proposing his theory of the positive and the
negative emotion, and more especially the theory of the

---

[3] I have inserted here W. Rhys Roberts' translation of καθ' ὑπεναντιώσεις
because it conveys more accurately the force of the Greek, which means
*opposite feelings* rather than "at variance within," as Granger has it.

[4] Roberts has it "a concourse of passions," which is more accurate. The Greek
ἵνα μὴ ἕν τι περὶ αὐτὴν πάθος φαίνηται, παθῶν δὲ σύνοδος is literally a "coming together of roads," a crossroads; so better perhaps than
either "their whole company" or a "concourse of passions" are the rendi-
tions "a clash of feelings," "a crossing of feelings."

central "emotion" gathering up and controlling a variety of contingent "feelings." Mr. Eliot's early theory I should call advanced romantic criticism: it was struggling through the subjective effect towards the objective structure of the work. Longinus' criticism of Sappho is advanced romantic criticism, as advanced as Mr. Eliot's.

One hesitates to present to Longinus a theory which I hope is not implicit in his phrase ἕν τι σῶμα ποιεῖν, "to make into one body"; it looks like an organic theory of poetry, but if we suppose that he is merely using the phrase analogically, and means by it no more than he says a moment later about the poem being a result of choosing and binding together intense feelings, we shall have to acknowledge the presence of a quite modern piece of criticism. At the least, he is telling us that in this poem contradictions are united, bound together, not that Sappho was expressing herself. We are a long step on the way to that critical moment when the affective vocabulary goes over into linguistic analysis, when, instead of what the poem feels like, we try to decide what it says. That Longinus was farther along this road than we may at a glance suspect there is evidence in the remarkable sentence that he plumps down before us without explanation: ". . . the sublime is often found where there is no emotion." There will be something to say about this when we come to the discussion of "harmony," or composition.

## V

The promise at the beginning of the treatise to produce the elements of an Art of Elevation leads to a good deal of miscellaneous specification, under five heads, for its achievement; but the dialectical links among the categories are not distinct. If we think of Longinus as Pascal's man of *finesse*, man of insights, and of Aristotle as a man of *géométrie*, man of deduction, we shall have to look twice at Mr. Olson's observation that, "Unlike Edmund Burke, who finds the sources of sublimity in qualities of the subject matter of art, Longinus finds them in the faculties of the author." This is partly true; but it is misleading, if we are led to suppose that Longinus tried but failed to erect a systematic philosophy of art, comparable to Burke's *A Philosophical Enquiry into the Origins of Our Ideas of the Sublime and Beautiful*, but placing the origin of the ideas in the author. He is ambiguous at this point, but I have shown, I hope, that his considerable originality consists in shifting the center of critical interest, without rejecting it as an "interest," from the genetic and moral judgment to the aesthetic, from the subject matter and the psychology of the author to the language of the work. When he describes the first of his five sources of Elevation as the "impulse towards what is great in thought," he speaks perhaps as a casual Platonist, but primarily as a rhetorician in the great tradition reaching from Aristotle to Cicero.

In distinguishing a critical insight from the intellectual discipline from which, to an extent, it may be a departure, we tend to assume that the insight has replaced the discipline; whereas it may merely alter it. It is not certain that we need a philosophical aesthetics in order to produce a work of art; at the Renaissance, I need hardly to observe, the education in rhetoric and oratory produced poets. Sidney is not too apologetic for "straying from Poetrie to Oratorie"; for, he says, "both have such an affinity in this wordish consideration. . . ." It was the point of view of his age. Disciplining that point of view was the art of rhetoric, one member of a tripartite whole completed by ethics and politics; rhetoric was the ethics of the public man in its appropriate discipline, the art of the enthymeme, or rhetorical syllogism.

The second of Longinus' categories, "strong and inspired emotion," proceeds from the first, or from a common source; it also is "due to nature." Here we come upon a curious and, as usual, undeveloped observation. Strong and inspired emotion is one source of, but it is not the same as, style. Pity, grief, and fear, he says, are "humble [ταπεινά : lowly, mean] and without the note of the Sublime" — as if in "pity" and "fear" he had a critical eye to Aristotle, whose doctrine of *katharsis* was practical and even "sociological." The curious observation honors the critic who puts "awareness" above system, for it enters an exception to the rule: "The masters of panegyric," Longinus says, "are seldom given to emotion." What, then, are they given to? An English instance will be helpful. The epigraph to "Lycidas" tells us that "The Author bewails a Learned Friend" — but the author does nothing of the sort;[5] the strong feeling is directed at the clergy, and even it is sufficiently assimilated into the rich pastoral texture.

I pass over sources two and three, the "framing of rhetorical figures" and "nobility of expression," with the remark that Longinus is prudential, like a good teacher, and on these topics not more rewarding than the rhetoricians, Demetrius and Dionysius. But number five, "Composition and distribution of words and phrases into a dignified and exalted unit," heads up the entire argument. "It is a unity of composition," he says, "attained through language." If it is so attained, it is not attained, though it may originate, in the inaccessible nobility of the author's mind. Observe again the superiority of Longinus' insight, with the specific work in mind, to his critical apparatus, which tends to the moralistic and academic. We may see composition here as *ordonnance*, "the best words in the best order." It is more than that. Composition is the total work, not the superaddition of method. Its effect is not to persuade but to entrance; it is "out of the common," not uncommon words, but words used uncommonly well. It is clear that Longinus, by and large, is not recommending the "grand style"; his transla-

[5] Mr. John Crowe Ransom made this observation in "A Poem Nearly Anonymous," *The World's Body* (Scribner, 1938), pp. 1-28.

tors have probably done him a disservice in rendering his characteristic adjective μέγα as "grand"; it is, rather, great, unusual, *uncommon;* and likewise ὕψος, "height," which I understand as "excellence." ἔκστασις is our subjective acknowledgement of the presence of the uncommon, of an objective order of unpredictable distinction. He is quite explicit in this matter. By means of "an appropriate structure, and by this means only, as we have sufficiently shown, the best writers give the effect of stateliness and distinction which is removed from the commonplace." In illustration he quotes a line from the *Hercules Furens* of Euripides:

γέμω κακῶν δὴ κοὐκετ᾽ ἔσθ᾽ ὅποι τεθῇ,

*I am loaded with sorrows nor can I take on more.*

"The phrase is quite commonplace but it has *gained elevation* by the arrangement of the words." The fine statement that follows ought to remove any remaining misconception of the nature of "transport," if we still suppose it to be the romantic shudder; it addresses itself to the whole mind:

> . . . if a work of literature fails to disclose to the reader's intelligence an outlook beyond the range of what is said, when it dwindles under a careful and continuous inspection, it cannot be truly sublime, for it has reached the ear alone. . . . For that is truly grand [μέγα] of which the contemplation bears repeating.

There must be, in short, a total quality of the work which abides its first impact; to that total quality he gives the name of composition.

It includes rhythm. Saintsbury, whose exposition of Longinus might have revived his influence had somebody else written it, misses the originality of Longinus' treatment of this subject. Longinus' location of rhythm in the total composition, as binding and bound up with it, is perhaps the best critical insight of its kind before Coleridge. Quoting a passage from Demosthenes, he makes the experiment of adding a syllable, and observes that the "sublime phrase is loosened and undone by lengthening of the final rhythm." Likewise, if the phrase were shortened by a syllable. His principle of prose rhythm is negatively stated, but it seems to me to hold for every kind of writing. It is: prose rhythm should not have "a conspicuous movement of sound." It must seem, even if metaphysically it is not, at one with the meaning; it must not call attention to itself, unless — as in Tacitus, Gibbon, Doughty, or Sir Thomas Browne — the "conspicuous movement of sound" is a tonal vehicle that once established is not distinguishable from, but is a part of, the subject itself. But if it is a rhythm "like that of a dancer taking his step before the audience," which the audience anticipates, it distracts attention from what is being said to who is saying it. It is a disproportion in composition similar to that of the orator or the poet who "digresses from the subject into his own tedious emotions." Had Longinus been discussing the rhythm of verse, I should have been able to cite Swinburne and *The Age of Anxiety* by Mr. W. H. Auden.

## VI

I have postponed consideration of the third source of Elevation to this concluding section because it pertains in part to metaphor, the *pons asinorum* of literary criticism. If on this subject Longinus is unsatisfactory, it is only a matter of degree; here everybody is unsatisfactory, even Mr. I. A. Richards, whose *Philosophy of Rhetoric* offers a good deal but promises too much. This is a field of inquiry of a difficulty co-ordinate with that of the burden of the mystery. Here again Longinus is prudential, but he no doubt gives us as good an account as any of the classical precept of nothing-too-much. Don't use too many metaphors, unless you are overwhelmed by emotions which may make them credible. Follow Aristotle, perhaps in the *Rhetoric;* soften the metaphor up by inserting "as if" or "just as though" and making it a simile that does not assert improbable identities.

One goes through the περὶ ὕψους, and then the *Rhetoric,* half-heartedly and vainly, looking for something better than this, from the literary point of view, that Longinus might have overlooked, or for something as far-reaching as Aristotle's own Delphic pronouncement in Chapter XXII of the *Poetics,* where he says:

> It is a great thing indeed to make a proper use of these poetical forms, as also of compounds and strange words. But the greatest thing by far is to be a master of metaphor. It is the one thing that cannot be learnt

from others; and it is also a sign of genius, since a good
metaphor implies an intuitive perception of the similar-
ity in dissimilars.

That is very nearly the beginning and the end of our own
inquiries into metaphor; but I am rash enough to question
whether Aristotle, as a Greek, could know, as we have known
since Shakespeare and Donne, how similar dissimilars can
be made to seem, or (to take an extreme view which is not
unknown today) how similar they can be made to *be*. Metaphor, says Aristotle, is the transference of names, through
the permutations of genus and species, or by analogy.
Metaphor by analogy takes the formula of arithmetical
proportion, a quantitative and relational procedure. We are
thus in the Greek Cosmos, an ordering of solid objects under
a physics of motion, in which the formal object offers but a
narrow margin of analogy to any other. If the ancient inquiry into the structure of metaphor was less resourceful
than ours, it was not I daresay because Aristotle was less
intelligent than the best modern critics. Our multiverse has
increasingly, since the seventeenth century, consisted of
unstable objects dissolving into energy; and there has been
no limit to the extension of analogy. Criticism follows
whatever it is given to follow. Are the famous lucidity and
the restraint of the Greeks evidence that by nature they were
more lucid and more restrained than we? I doubt it. For
even the physical sight may be controlled by the religious
selectivity, which fixes the height and the direction of the

casement framing our inspection of the world. To introduce at the end of an essay so large and so undeveloped a conception is an impropriety of length and occasion; I offer it as historical relativism in defense of Longinus and of ourselves.

On no single kind of literature is Longinus as searching as Aristotle on tragedy. But I risk the guess that he came nearer to a comprehensive theory of literary form than any other ancient critic. If he did not quite make the leap to a complete theory of the language of imagination, we must remember that nobody in the ancient world did. He shared Aristotle's cosmetic sense of the simple relation between word and thing; in a world of fixed forms, thing was unyielding; the word, like its object, retained a plastic visibility. With the Greeks the "transference" of "names" was limited to the surface designation, to the comparison of objects in the round, to sculpturesque analogy. Metaphor was a feature of discourse to be described, not a metaphysical problem to be investigated. We need not see as a personal limitation Longinus' failure to investigate a problem that for him did not exist. The permanent critics do not settle the question. They compel us to ask it again. They are the rotating chairmen of a debate only the rhetoric of which changes from time to time. Among these we may think of Longinus, if we will read him not in our age, but in his own.

*Herbert Read*

COLERIDGE AS CRITIC

*Herbert Read*

# COLERIDGE AS CRITIC

THE privilege of introducing Coleridge to a Symposium
devoted to "criticism" carries with it a certain act of
renunciation. There is no figure, in the whole history of
English literature, who is so intrinsically fascinating, and
we might spend a very pleasant hour recalling Coleridge's
personality in all its suggestiveness, its infinite variety, and,
to use his own word, its *multeity*. There is an entry in the
recently published *Notebooks* of Henry James which well
expresses this fatal attractiveness. That connoisseur in character, in dramatic situations, in psychological subtleties,
had been reading the then recently published biography of
Coleridge by Dykes Campbell, and he says that he

> was infinitely struck with the suggestiveness of S.T.C.'s
> figure — wonderful, admirable figure — for pictorial
> treatment. What a subject some particular cluster of
> its relations would make for a little story, a small vivid
> picture. There was a point, as I read, at which I seemed
> to see a little story — to have a quick glimpse of the
> possible drama. Would not such a drama necessarily
> be the question of the acceptance by someone — some-

one with something important at stake — of the general *responsibility* of rising to the height of accepting him for what he is, recognizing his rare, anomalous, magnificent, interesting, curious, tremendously suggestive character, vices and all, with all its imperfections on its head, and *not* being guilty of the pedantry, the stupidity, the want of imagination, of fighting him, deploring him in the details — failing to recognize that one *must* pay for him and that on the whole he is magnificently worth it.[1]

From that particular suggestion emerged, eventually, one of James's best stories — "The Coxon Fund." Though our aims are so different, and have no dramatic effect in view, yet the injunctions that Henry James proposed to himself are not altogether inapplicable. In particular, we must accept Coleridge for what he was, not merely as a person, but as an intellect, "vices and all"; and we must not be guilty of a partial portrait, of a selection of evidence designed to present a critic merely congenial — a critic of little vivid perceptions, of penetrating insight — to the neglect of all that constituted the real substance and capacity of the man and his mind.* [The danger is a real one, and has not been avoided by writers on Coleridge. We need not, I think, take too seriously those who try to dissociate the poet and the

---

[1] *The Notebooks of Henry James,* ed. F. O. Matthiessen and Kenneth B. Murdock (New York, 1947), p. 152.

* The passages in square brackets were omitted from the lecture as delivered at the Symposium.

philosopher. An eminent dichotomist of this school was the late Sir Arthur Quiller-Couch, who put forward the suggestion that Coleridge was a poet up to the moment he went to Germany, a young man of twenty-six. "He landed in Germany," writes Sir Arthur, "a poet; and a poet, so to speak, with his hand in; his mind flushed with recent poetic feats, quick with poetry to come. He embarked from Germany . . . a poet lost . . . came back to England intensely and furiously preoccupied with metaphysics. *This*," suggests Sir Arthur, "this and neither opium nor Mrs. Coleridge's fretfulness, was the main reason why he could not recall his mind to poetry. . . ."[2]

Admittedly there is a psychological problem; for some reason Coleridge was henceforth to find it increasingly difficult to write poetry; and in that wonderful but pathetic Ode: *Dejection*, which he wrote in his thirtieth year, and in which he openly confessed the failing of his "genial spirits," he carried the psychological analysis of his mental state to a point of realistic revelation which no external investigator is ever likely to improve on. This Ode must be read in its original form, first published by Professor Ernest de Selincourt in 1937, for there Coleridge reveals the real source of his affliction:

> . . . *my coarse domestic Life has known*
> *No Habits of heart-nursing Sympathy,*
> *No Griefs but such as dull and deaden me,*

2 Introduction to *Biographia Literaria,* ed. G. Sampson (Cambridge, 1920).

*No mutual mild Enjoyments of its own,*
*No Hopes of its own Vintage, None O! none —*
*Whence when I mourn'd for you, my Heart might*
  *borrow*
*Fair forms and living Motions for its Sorrow.*[3]

and then come lines for long familiar, but which lost some of their force from being separated from the immediately preceding lines I have just quoted:

*For not to think of what I needs must feel,*
*But to be still and patient all I can;*
*And haply by abstruse Research to steal*
*From my own Nature, all the Natural man —*
*This was my sole Resource, my wisest plan!*
*And that, which suits a part, infects the whole,*
*And now is almost grown the temper of my soul.*

Writing in this same year in 1802, about four months after the composition of this Ode, Coleridge confessed to Southey that

all my poetic genius (if ever I really possessed any *genius*, and it was not rather a more general aptitude of talent and quickness in imitation) is gone, and I have been fool enough to suffer deeply in my mind, regretting the loss, which I attribute to my long and exceedingly severe metaphysical investigations, and these partly to ill-health, and partly to private afflic-

[3] The complete text is given by de Selincourt in his *Wordsworthian and Other Studies* (Oxford, 1947), pp. 67-76.

tions which rendered any subjects, immediately connected with feeling, a source of pain and disquiet
to me.[4]

At first sight this might seem to confirm Sir Arthur Quiller-
Couch's theory, that metaphysics destroyed the poet in Coleridge. But in another letter written only sixteen days earlier,
Coleridge had said: "Metaphysics is a word that you, my
dear sir, are not a great friend to, but yet you will agree with
me that a great poet must be *implicité*, if not *explicité*, a profound metaphysician";[5] and there is that still more uncom-
promising statement in the *Biographia Literaria*: "No man
was ever yet a great poet, without being at the same time a
profound philosopher."[6] The greatest poetry, as we shall
see when we come to discuss Coleridge's theory of poetry,
is precisely that in which "the creative power and the intellectual energy wrestle as in a war embrace."

The truth of the matter is, I think, that the concentration
demanded by metaphysical investigations is a better ano-
dyne for private afflictions than poetry, for in poetry the
emotions are involved. But this does not imply, and Coleridge never for a moment entertained the idea, that metaphysics was foreign to poetry, or destructive of poetic genius.
Coleridge repeatedly asserts that but for his afflictions he
would have made it his business to embody his philosophy

[4] Letters (1895), I, 388.
[5] *Ibid.*, 372.
[6] *Biographia Literaria*, ed. John Shawcross (Oxford, 1907), II, 19.

in his poetry, more exactly, to make poetry an instrument of metaphysical research.]

It will already be evident that I am going to make it one of my main concerns in this lecture to defend the philosopher in Coleridge. It would be outside my scope, and, indeed, beyond my capacity, to defend Coleridge's philosophy as such. But I shall try to show the relevance of the philosophy to the criticism and further, and in this departing from most predecessors in this field, I shall maintain that the criticism was deepened — was, indeed, given another and greater dimension, by its dependence on a definite philosophical method.

Writing in 1840, six years after Coleridge's death, John Stuart Mill expressed the opinion that

> the class of thinkers has scarcely yet arisen by whom [Coleridge as a philosopher] is to be judged. The limited philosophical public of this country is as yet too exclusively divided between those to whom Coleridge and the views which he promulgated or defended are everything, and those to whom they are nothing. A true thinker can only be justly estimated when his thoughts have worked their way into minds formed in a different school; have been wrought and moulded into consistency with all other true and relevant thoughts; when the noisy conflict of half-truths, angrily denying one another, has subsided, and ideas which seemed mutually incompatible, have been found only

to require mutual limitations. This time has not yet
come for Coleridge.[7]

The transcendental philosophy, of which Coleridge was
a late but brilliant luminary, has long ago taken its due place
in the historical perspective of philosophy. Certain subsequent schools, of which the most contentious have been
Hegelianism, dialectical materialism, positivism, and pragmatism, have obscured for a time the originality and perennial force of that mansion of thought whose foundations
were laid by Kant, whose glittering pinnacles were completed by Coleridge, Novalis, and Kierkegaard. I must speak
with caution in a country where pragmatism, I am told, is
still regarded as the national philosophy; but if I am not
mistaken, here as well as in Europe there has been in recent
years a return to a more idealistic attitude in philosophy.
This is shown in the remarkable interest now shown in
Kierkegaard, and in the spread of a philosophy which, in
some three distinct varieties, is known as *existentialism*. It
will become evident as we proceed that Coleridge, no less
than Kierkegaard, comes within the range of this revivalism.

Much research has been devoted to the origins of Coleridge's philosophy, and a controversy, not lacking in ani-
mosity, has continued from Coleridge's own day to our own.
There has been a charge, not merely of derivation, but even
of dishonest plagiarism, to which the untidy literary habits

[7] *London and Westminster Review* (March, 1840), reprinted in *Dissertations
and Discussions*, Vol. I (1867), pp. 397-8.

of Coleridge yielded only too much evidence. Coleridge himself was aware of this accusation, and showed himself rightly sensitive to the imputation of dishonesty. He did his best to answer the charge, and in various contexts made generous admission of his debts. I do not wish to spend any time going over the well-trodden grounds of this dispute, but it is desirable, for my purpose, to establish the main sources of Coleridge's philosophy — to allot the credits, as they say in Hollywood.

Coleridge was a polymath. He took all knowledge for his province, and from the day when "the old Grey Friars re-echoed to the accents of the *inspired charity-boy*," as his schoolmate Charles Lamb called him, "the young Miran-dula, waxing, even in those early years, not pale at philo-sophic draughts of Jamblichus or Plotinus," from that day until his death Coleridge continued to absorb knowledge from all quarters. He never lost his zest for learning, and a list of authors and works quoted in his writings would in itself fill a volume. It is never safe to assume that Coleridge had not read anything published before the year of his death. I remember my astonishment in discovering that he had read Vico's *Scienza Nuova*, long before Michelet rescued that great name from oblivion.[8] When we say that Coleridge took

---

[8] It was lent to him by an Italian lawyer called Dr. de Prati. See *Unpub-lished Letters*, II, 374. He was reading it when, in 1825, he paid a visit to Ramsgate, as we learn from the following characteristic note in a letter to Gillman: "To Margate, and saw the caverns, as likewise smelt the same, called on Mr. Bailey, and got the *Novum Organum*. In my hurry, I scram-bled up the *Blackwood* instead of a volume of Giovanni Battista Vico,

all knowledge for his province, we must insist on the literal
meaning of the phrase. It is not always remembered what
a part the natural sciences played in his development. His
main motive in going to Germany in 1798, apart from acquiring proficiency in the language, was to study chemistry
and anatomy, mechanics and optics, philology and ethnol-
ogy. His appetite was inordinate, his ambitions sublime.

> I should not think [he wrote to Cottle] of devoting less
> than twenty years to an epic poem. Ten years to collect
> materials and warm my mind with universal science. I
> would thoroughly understand Mechanics; Hydrostat-
> ics; Optics and Astronomy; Botany; Metallurgy;
> Fossilism; Chemistry; Geology; Anatomy; Medicine;
> then the mind of man; then the minds of Men, in all
> Travels, Voyages and Histories. So I would spend ten
> years; the next five in the composition of the poem, and
> the last five in the correction of it. So would I write,
> haply not unhearing of that divine and nightly-whis-
> pering voice, which speaks to mighty minds, of pre-
> destinated garlands, starry and unwithering.[9]

Alas, "that divine and nightly-whispering voice" was to fail
him, but there is no doubt that he carried out the first part of
this programme. At Göttingen he took courses, not only in
German language and literature, but also in physiology and

which I left on the table in my room, and forgot my sponge and sponge-bag
of oiled silk. But perhaps when I sit down to work, I may have to request
something to be sent, which may come with them." *Letters*, II, 744.

[9] *Biographia Epistolaris*, I, 130 (May, 1797).

natural history. The study of philosophy was for a time postponed, but not forgotten; for Coleridge came back from Germany with £30 of "metaphysical" books, and it was these which were destined to have a decisive influence on his own philosophy.

In assessing the relative importance of these influences it is well to have some regard to Coleridge's own statements, which often betray a significant emphasis. There is no doubt that the year in Germany was a decisive watershed in his intellectual development. The impact of the systematic atmosphere of a German university — and, one might say, the impact of a nation in a state of vivid intellectual awareness — all this sufficed to make him realize that in his previous studies he had merely floundered — that his head was stored with "crude notions." What these crude notions were we know well: they were the product of a rapid and uncritical absorption of such mutually incompatible philosophies as those represented, on the one hand, by Plato and the Neoplatonists, Christian mystics like Jacob Böhme and William Law, the English divines and theologians, and, on the other hand, the much more sceptical tradition of Locke, Hume, Voltaire, Condillac, and Hartley. In the midst of these contending forces, Coleridge had held on to what he called "an exclusive consciousness of God," a faith, the consequence of a deliberate act of the will, enlightened by intuition, but defiant of the logical processes of the intellect. He had held on to this rock of faith, but there is no doubt that, at the time he went to Germany, his mind was "perplexed." He remained, as he says in the *Biographia Literaria*, a zealous Unitarian; he considered the *idea* of the Trinity a fair inference from the being of God; but he had doubts about the Incarnation, the redemption by the Cross, and many other matters of doctrine. "A more thorough revolution in my philosophic principles, and a deeper insight into my own heart, were yet wanting" — such was his own analysis of the situation.[10]

It is tempting to consider how those doubts were resolved, but I must not be led astray from my main topic, which is Coleridge's critical philosophy. But Coleridge only established a critical philosophy as part of his general philosophy, and his critical activity cannot fairly be separated from his metaphysical activity — in fact, the epithet "critical," in his case as in Kant's, is rather more important than the substantive "philosophy." The "critique" is a method of indirect affirmation. Kant felt that he could best establish the truth by criticizing the methods of reasoning, especially those used by Hume. We shall see that Coleridge made the criticism of *method* the basis of his aesthetics.

What Coleridge owed to the critical philosophy of Kant, or to the transcendentalists as a school, cannot be established accurately. Let us realize, once and for all, that we are not dealing with the scholarly lucubrations of an academic coterie, in which priorities and credits are of some impor-

[10] *Biographia Literaria*, I, 137.

tance. Coleridge was involved in something much wider and
more fundamental — in a revolution of thought such as only
occurs once or twice in a millennium. Such revolutions do
not come about as a result of individual efforts: the individuals are swept along in a current which they, least of all
men, can control. Kant's philosophy is inconceivable without the stimulus of Hume; Fichte is inconceivable without
Kant, and Schelling without Fichte. Let us rather visualize
this whole movement of thought as a fleet of vessels moving
towards new and uncharted seas. Kant and Fichte, Schleier-
macher and Schelling; Herder and the two Schlegels;
Goethe and Schiller; Tieck, Novalis, and Wackenroder —
so many vessels advancing in the stream of thought, flashing
signals from one masthead to another, and all guided on
their way by the lodestar of transcendental truth. As they
proceed from some harbor in the Baltic, they are joined by
solitary vessels from neighboring countries, and Coleridge
is one of these, already armed and provisioned, his course
set to the same destination.

Of his fellow voyagers, Coleridge was to select two for
closest alliance. We need not dismiss his obligations to the
Schlegels, nor to Lessing and Schiller (Schiller in particular
offers a correspondence of *aim*, as of endowments, which
bring him into close sympathy). But Coleridge himself, by
the warmth and fullness of his acknowledgments, gave fullest credit to Kant and Schelling. He said of Kant that he had
taken possession of him "as with the giant's hand"; that he

had "at once invigorated and disciplined" his understanding; and after fifteen years' familiarity with his works, he still read them "with undiminished delight and unceasing admiration."[11] That is humble discipleship; but towards Schelling, to whom his acknowledgments were equally full, he indicated a somewhat different, and perhaps more significant relationship. "In Schelling," he said, "I first found a genial coincidence with much that I had toiled out for myself, and a powerful assistance *in what I had yet to do.*" What had yet to be done was the application of Kant's dynamic philosophy to one or two spheres which had only been vaguely indicated by the master. Of his followers, with the partial exception of Fichte, only Schelling, in Coleridge's view, had succeeded in completing the system, in consolidating its victories. In what remained to be done, the application of the system to "the most awful of subjects for the most important of purposes," only Schelling's aid was of any real value.

[Let us try and recall — very briefly, for my time is nearly half spent — the significant links between Kant and Schelling, and then see how Coleridge added to them. A drastic simplification will be necessary.]

The exceptional nature of aesthetic judgments — that is

11 *Biographia Literaria,* I, 99. Cf. *Letters,* 682. ". . . I reverence Kant with my whole heart and soul and believe him to be the only philosopher, for *all men* who have the power of thinking. I cannot conceive the liberal pursuit or profession, in which the service derived from a patient study of his works would not be incalculably great, both as cathartic, tonic, and directly nutritious."

to say, of the mental experience involved whenever a distinction of inherent value or worth is made between one work of art and another — was first recognized by Leibnitz. But there it remained — an anomaly unaccounted for — until Kant, in his *Critique of Judgment,* established a connection between the formal purposiveness of nature and the creative freedom of the artist. Kant did not venture beyond the suggestion of various analogies — beauty, for example, becomes the *symbol* of morality, and the creative activity in art the dynamic counterpart of the teleological principle of the universe. Kant was not himself an artist; he had no inner experience of the creative activity, and his use of illustrative material is conventional and uncertain. But Schelling, whose ambition it was to complete the transcendental philosophy, though perhaps not a very good poet, was at any rate a man of sensibility, with a keen appreciation of all the arts. On the basis of this appreciative knowledge he ventured to go a step beyond Kant, to pass from mere analogies to absolute identification. Art becomes "the only true and enduring organon and document of philosophy" — "the keystone of its entire arch." He imagined, as basic to the universe, an energy, or creative impulse which, when unconscious, is manifested as nature; when conscious, as art.

[The objective world, which is unconscious, becomes conscious in the subjective activity of the ego — the conscious and the unconscious meet and are unified in the state of consciousness.] The ideal work of art and the real world

of objects are products of one and the same aesthetic activity. Art is the only permanent revelation of the nature of
reality. He asks us to think of nature as a poem hidden in
a secret and mysterious writing. If the secret could be revealed, we should find that it was an odyssey of the human
spirit; but the more we strive after its meaning, the more
elusive it becomes. The senses, which are our only key, are
baffled by a veil of words. It is like trying to get a glimpse
of fairyland through fleeting clouds. A painting, too, which
only comes to life when the veil between the real and the
ideal world is lifted, is merely an aperture through which
are projected the forms of the world of the imagination,
which in its turn is a shimmering reflection of the real world.
For the artist nature is much the same as it is for the philosopher — the ideal world manifesting itself under continual
limitations. It is the incomplete reflection of a world that
exists, not outside but within the artist.[12] This, admittedly, is
still a very metaphorical manner of philosophizing, and a
contemporary like Schiller, who had more practical experience of the poetic activity, rightly accused Schelling of
putting the cart before the horse. Poetry, he pointed out,
sets out from the unconscious, and its difficulty consists in
knowing how to realize, to make actual, the vague intima-
tions that the poet derives from his unconscious, without at
the same time sacrificing the vitality of the inspiration. The
poet somehow has to manage to combine thought and sensi-

[12] Cf. *System des transcendentalen Idealismus* (1800), pp. 475-6.

bility, intuition and reflection.[13] Coleridge's point of departure from Schelling is of exactly the same nature.

If we were considering Coleridge as a philosopher, rather than as a critic, we should have to trace his relationship to Schelling in much more detail; but enough, perhaps, has been said to establish a necessary connection. The distinction of Coleridge, which puts him head and shoulders above every other English critic, is due to his introduction of a philosophical method of criticism. English criticism before his time, in the hands of a Dryden, a Warton, or a Johnson, had been a criticism of technique, of craftsmanship — sometimes presupposing some general rules, such as that of dramatic unity, but oftener a merely mechanical, and at best an individualistic and arbitrary activity, resulting in such perversities, or rather inadequacies, as Johnson's remarks

[13] Schiller, like Coleridge, always referred his theories to his own practical experience as a poet. Cf. his illuminating criticism of Schelling in a letter to Goethe (March 27, 1801): "He assumes that, in the realm of nature, one should take as a point of departure what is without consciousness, in order to attain to consciousness; whilst, in the realm of art, one sets out from consciousness to attain the unconscious. . . . I am afraid that these idealists do not profit much from experience; for experience teaches that the poet's unique point of departure is in the unconscious; I would even say that the poet should count himself lucky if he succeeds, more or less, while making use of a consciousness fully aware of its mode of operation, in recovering in the finished work, unattenuated, the first and still obscure total idea which he had conceived of his work. Lacking such a total idea, obscure but powerful, anterior to all technical apparatus, it is not possible for any poetic work to be born; and poetry, if I am not mistaken, consists precisely in knowing how to express and communicate this unconscious — in other words, in knowing how to embody it in an objective work of art." The whole letter deserves careful reading, for like everything that Schiller wrote on aesthetic theory, it is full of wise perceptions and anticipations of later theories of art.

on Shakespeare. Coleridge changed all that. He himself observed:

> The science of Criticism dates its restoration from the time when it was seen that an examination and appreciation of the end was necessarily antecedent to the formation of the rules, supplying at once the principle of the rules themselves, and of their application to the given subject. From this time we have heard little (among intelligent persons, I mean) of the wildness and irregularity of our Shakespeare. Nay, when once the end which our myriad-minded Bard had in view, and the local accidents that favoured or obstructed or in any way modified its manifestations are once thoroughly comprehended, the doubt will arise whether the judgment or the genius of the man has the stronger claim to our wonder, or rather it will be felt that the judgment was the birth and living offspring of his genius even as the symmetry of a body results from the sanity and vigour of the life as an organizing power.[14]

The "method" that Coleridge introduced into criticism is expounded in a series of brilliant essays which make up the Second Section of *The Friend*, one of the few parts of his work on which Coleridge himself looked back with any satisfaction.[15] Method is said to become natural

---

[14] M.S. *Logic*. Cf. Alice D. Snyder, *Coleridge on Logic and Learning* (Yale, 1929), p. 110.

[15] "Were it in my power, my works should be confined to the second volume of my 'Literary Life,' the Essays of the third volume of the 'Friend' (Sec-

to the mind which has become accustomed to contemplate not things only, or for their own sake alone, but likewise and chiefly the relations of things, either their relations to each other, or to the observer, or to the state and apprehension of the hearers. To enumerate and analyze these relations, with the conditions under which alone they are discoverable is to teach the science of method.[16]

To avoid the impression that method is merely a sterile system of classification, Coleridge illustrated its meaning from the art of Shakespeare. He sees it as "The unpremeditated and evidently habitual arrangement of . . . words, grounded on the habit of foreseeing, in each integral part, or (more plainly) in every sentence, the whole that [the poet] then intends to communicate."[17] Mrs. Quickly's relation of the circumstances of Sir John Falstaff's debt to her is given as Shakespeare's illustration of the want of method in the uneducated; and the habitual use of method is shown by contrast in Hamlet's account of the events which accompanied his proposed transportation to England. Then, making further use of this same illustration, Coleridge shows how an "exuberance of mind . . . interferes with the forms of method; but sterility of mind . . . wanting the spring and

tion II), with about fifty or sixty pages from the two former volumes, and some half-dozen of my poems." Letter to J. Britton (Feb. 28, 1819). Cf. Raysor, *Shakespearean Criticism*, Vol. II, p. 326.

16 *The Friend* (4th edn., 1850), III, 108.

17 *Ibid.*, p. 104.

impulse to mental action, is wholly destructive of method itself.[18] "The terms system, method, science, are mere improprieties of courtesy, when applied to a mass enlarging by endless appositions, but without a nerve that oscillates, or a pulse that throbs, in sign of growth or inward sympathy."[19] He brings this analysis down to a significant point — significant, I mean, for Coleridge's whole philosophy — the necessity, in all mental processes, for "a staple, or starting-post, in the narrator himself." Mental confusion is due to "the absence of the leading thought, which," (and here Coleridge is introducing one of the terms which have since become current in literary criticism) "borrowing a phrase from the nomenclature of legislation, I may not inaptly call the initiative." Granted a starting-post, then "things most remote and diverse in time, place, and outward circumstance, are brought into mental contiguity and succession, the more striking as the less expected."[20] But the method must not be stretched into despotism — that way lies the grotesque and the fantastical. "Confusion and formality are but the opposite poles of the same null-point." Method, true method, implies "a progressive transition," and for a transition to be continuous there must be a preconception. Thus in Shakespeare, "in all his various characters, we still feel ourselves communicating with the same nature, which is

18 *Ibid.*, p. 112.
19 *Ibid.*, p. 132.
20 *Ibid.*, p. 113.

everywhere present as the vegetable sap in the branches, sprays, leaves, buds, blossoms, and fruits, their shapes, tastes, and odours." The excellence of Shakespeare consists in "that just proportion, that union and interpenetration, of the universal and particular, which must ever pervade all works of decided genius and true science."[21]

Coleridge reveals his debt to Kant and Schelling in all that follows, but he is everywhere giving the critical method his own application. He distinguishes between two kinds of relation — that of *law* (which is the Kantian conception of the category, of the truth originating in the mind) and that of *theory*, which is the relation of cause and effect, leading to the generalizations of science, the arrangement of the many under one point of view. Between these two relations, says Coleridge, lies method in the fine arts, which is partly a synthetical activity based on knowledge and experience, but this activity dominated by the intuitive conceptions of the artist. Coleridge described the process by means of which this domination is achieved as "esemplastic," a word which has never taken root in our language. Whatever he might call it, he always had in mind his own creative experience as a poet, and it is that fact which gives a sense of realism to all his theorizing. In this he was but following his own maxim, to the effect that in order to recognize his place in nature, man must first learn to comprehend nature in himself, and its laws in the grounds of his own existence. In this

21 *Ibid.*, p. 116.

spirit Coleridge becomes the first psychologist in criticism —
he was, indeed, the first literary critic to make use of the
very word "psychology."

This psychological analysis of the workings of the poetic
process in himself, and, so far as external examination could
yield the facts, of the same process in his friend Wordsworth,
led Coleridge to formulate what I would call *the romantic
principle in art*. To this principle he gave several formula-
tions, but the substance of them does not vary. From Schelling he had got the idea that art was "a dim analogue of
creation"; but creation itself was the process to be rendered
a little less dim. In the separate tasks assigned to himself
and Wordsworth in the composition of the *Lyrical Ballads*,
while Wordsworth was to "consider the influences of fancy
and imagination as they are manifested in poetry," Coleridge's task was "to investigate the seminal principle" itself.
Wordsworth was to sketch "the branches with their *poetic*
fruitage"; Coleridge "to add the trunk, and even the roots
as far as they lift themselves above the ground, and are
visible to the naked eye of our common consciousness."[22]

Professor Raysor, whose editorial work on Coleridge has
put us all under a great debt, has described Coleridge's
theory of the imagination as "eccentric" and "unfortunate";
and Coleridge himself as "a mediocre philosopher."[23] I do
not know from what more positive standpoint Professor

[22] *Biographia Literaria*, I, 64.
[23] *Shakespearean Criticism*, p. xxxiii n., xlviii n.

Raysor is criticizing the critic and philosopher to whom he
has given such loving care; but from my own standpoint I
must dissent from these strictures. Its terminology apart, I
believe that Coleridge's theory of the imagination has been
proved essentially sound by later and more scientific re-
searches, [and as for his philosophy, I hope in the little time
that is left to me to show that in this sphere, too, Coleridge,
so far from being mediocre, anticipated in many important
respects the point of view to which the philosophy of our
own time is busily returning.]

Coleridge was convinced that the imagination, in its highest potency, was something "essentially *vital*."[24] He also felt
that its source was in the unconscious — "There is in genius
itself," he said, "an unconscious activity; nay, that is *the*
genius in the man of genius."[25] What Coleridge meant by
the unconscious, and what Schelling meant by it, is not in
doubt; they both make frequent references to the unconscious activity of the dream, and they were both directly
influenced by Mesmer, from whose pioneer work on hypno-
sis developed, in good time, the whole theory of a dynamic
unconscious that Freud made the basis of his doctrine and
practice of psychoanalysis. For Coleridge, as for Schelling,
the unconscious was a reality of immense psychological
significance.[26]

24 *Biographia Literaria*, I, 202.
25 *Miscellaneous Criticism*, 210.
26 There is a beautiful illustration of his conception of the interaction of body
and mind at the end of Lecture XIII of the course of 1818 (*Miscellaneous*

The distinction between reason and understanding was, of course, of ancient origin; and Plato had been aware of the irrational sources of inspiration. But Fichte was perhaps the first philosopher to elaborate a threefold principle of knowledge. On the basis of Fichte's analysis, Schelling distinguished three "potencies." Again, I must stop on the threshold of metaphysics, but I think it can be stated, quite simply, that these three potencies of Schelling's represent, first, an irrational nonego or id; second, rational consciousness; and finally, a development of rational consciousness into a higher form of subjective consciousness. It has already been pointed out by an American scholar, Dr. Bolman, of Columbia, that Schelling's use of the three potencies in psychic life corresponds to Freud's threefold description of personality in terms of the id, the ego, and the superego.[27]

Now let us turn to Coleridge's theory of the imagination. He first tells us what the transcendental philosophy demands — first, that two forces should be conceived which contradict each other by their essential nature; secondly, that these forces should be assumed to be both alike infinite, both alike

*Criticism*, p. 213), repeated in the essay on "Poesy or Art." Cf. *Biographia Literaria*, Vol. II, p. 263. "The seeming identity of body and mind in infants, and thence the loveliness of the former. The commencing separation in boyhood, the struggle of equilibrium in youth; from thence onward the body first indifferent, then demanding the translucency of the mind not to be worse than indifferent; and finally, all that presents the body as body becoming almost of an excremental nature." In such a manner, perhaps, Schelling might have conceived his "Odysee des Geistes."

[27] Frederick de Wolfe Bolman, Jr., in his edition of Schelling's *The Ages of the World* (Columbia University Press, 1942), p. 166n.

indestructible. "The problem will then be to discover the result or product of two such forces, as distinguished from the result of those forces which are infinite. . . ." The next step is "to elevate the thesis from notional to actual, by contemplating intuitively this one power with its two inherent indestructible yet counteracting forces, and the results or generations to which their interpenetration gives existence, in the living principle and in the process of our own self-consciousness. By what instrument this is possible the solution itself will discover, at the same time that it will reveal to and for whom it is possible."[28]

The one power that issues from the interpenetration of these two assumed forces, Coleridge adds, is "inexhaustibly re-ebullient" — it cannot be neutralized, but must issue as a tertium quid, in finite generation. "This tertium quid can be no other than an interpenetration of the counteracting powers, partaking of both."[29]

Having delivered this flight into "High German Transcendentalism," Coleridge breaks off to interpose in his *Biographia Literaria* that "very judicious letter" from a friend "whose practical judgment I have ample reason to estimate and revere," namely himself; a letter in which he anticipates with humor and modesty the objections of those who, like Professor Raysor, regret his meddling in metaphysics — of the many, as he says, to whose minds his

28 *Biographia Literaria*, I, 197-8.
29 *Ibid.*, p. 198.

speculations on the esemplastic power will be utterly unin-
telligible. He then gives, in summary form, his famous definition of the Imagination, in its threefold potency, namely:

the *primary* imagination, the living Power and
Prime Agent of all human Perception;

the *secondary* imagination, an echo of the primary,
co-existing with the conscious will, yet still as identical
with the primary in the *kind* of its agency, and differing only in *degree*, and in the *mode* of its operation;

and finally the *fancy*, no other than a mode of memory emancipated from the order of time and place,
blended with and modified by that empirical phenomenon of the will, which we express by the word *choice*.

These summary definitions are amplified and illustrated
throughout the whole of Coleridge's literary criticism, and
it is my contention that that criticism derives its penetrative
power from the use of the systematic method he had established by his philosophical speculations. I have already mentioned the famous illustration of Shakespeare's poetic use
of method; illustrations of Coleridge's own critical use of
method abound in his lectures and miscellaneous writings.
One example will suffice — the blinding sword that he drives
between the talents of Beaumont and Fletcher and the genius
of Shakespeare:

What had a grammatical and logical consistency for
the ear, what could be put together and represented to
the eye, these poets [Beaumont and Fletcher] took

from the ear and eye, unchecked by any intuition of an
inward impossibility, just as a man might fit together
a quarter of an orange, a quarter of an apple, and the
like of a lemon and a pomegranate, and make it look
like one round diverse coloured fruit. But nature, who
works from within by evolution and assimilation according to a law, cannot do it. Nor could Shakespeare,
for he too worked in the spirit of nature, by evolving
the germ within by the imaginative power according
to an idea — for as the power of seeing is to light, so
is an idea in mind to a law in nature. They are correlatives that suppose each other.[30]

This, let me say in parenthesis, is one more statement of
what I have called the romantic principle — the idea that
the imagination is a shaping power, an energy which fuses,
melts, and recombines the elements of perception, and bodies
them forth in a unity or synthesis which is the work of art.
Coleridge everywhere insists on the difference between
"form as proceeding" and "shape as superinduced" — "the
latter is either the death or the imprisonment of the thing; —
the former is its self-witnessing and self-effected sphere of
agency." [And this, of course, is the precise difference between academic and romantic art.[31]]

30 *Miscellaneous Criticism*, pp. 42-3.
31 "On Poesy or Art." *Biographia Literaria*, II, 262. [I realize that in sub-
    stituting the word "academic" for the more usual word "classical" I am
    begging a question of a very debatable kind, but nothing is to be gained
    by accepting the misleading assumption that a historical distinction is
    at the same time a distinction of essence.]

But Coleridge, in his lecture on Beaumont and Fletcher, went on to make a further distinction that he regarded as of the utmost importance:

> Shakespeare shaped his characters out of the nature within; but we cannot so safely say, out of *his own* nature, as an *individual person*. No! this latter is itself but a *natura naturata*, an effect, a product, not a *power*. It was Shakespeare's prerogative to have the universal which is potentially in each *particular*, opened out to him in the *homo generalis*, not as an abstraction of observation from a variety of men, but as a substance capable of endless modifications, of which his own personal existence was but one, and to use *this one* as the eye that beheld the other, and as the tongue that could convey the discovery.[32]

[Here again Coleridge is anticipating the hypotheses of modern psychology, for what is clearly indicated in this passage is the conception of a *collective unconscious* to which the poet has special access, and of which he is the inspired exponent. Inspiration, however, is no arbitrary process; nor is beauty a copy of the mere externals of nature. The artist must master the essence, the *natura naturans*, "which presupposes a bond between nature in the highest sense and the soul of man." "Man's mind is the very focus of the rays of intellect which are scattered throughout the images of nature. Now so to place these images, totalized, and fitted to

[32] *Miscellaneous Criticism*, 43-4.

the limits of the human mind, as to elicit from, and to super-
induce upon, the forms themselves the moral reflexions to
which they approximate, to make the external internal, the
internal external, to make nature thought, and thought nature
— this is the mystery of genius in the Fine Arts."[33]]

The process might be illustrated in Coleridge's all too
brief references to the function of language in poetry. Coleridge realized, long before the theory of *Einfühlung* or
empathy had been formulated, that "to know is to resemble."
The artist "must imitate that which is within the thing, that
which is active through form and figure, and discourses to
us by symbols — the *Natur-geist*, or spirit of nature, as we
unconsciously imitate those we love, for so only can he hope
to produce any work truly natural in the object and truly
human in the effect. The idea which puts the form together
cannot itself be the form. It is above form, and is its essence,
the universal in the individual, or the individuality itself —
the glance and the exponent of the indwelling power."[34]
Following up this notion, there is a passage on language in
one of Coleridge's unpublished notebooks which runs:

> A man of Genius using a rich and expressive lan-
> guage (the Greek, German, or English) is an excellent
> instance and illustration of the ever individualizing
> process and dynamic Being, of Ideas. What a magnifi-
> cent History of acts of individual minds, sanctioned by

[33] "On Poesy or Art." *Biographia Literaria*, II, 257-8.
[34] *Ibid.*, 259.

the collective Mind of the Country, a Language is —
This Hint well deserves to be evolved and expounded
in a more auspicious moment. *Qy* whether words as the
already organized Materials of the higher Organic
Life . . . may not after a given period, become *effete?*
How rightly shall we conceive this marvellous Result,
a Language? — A chaos grinding itself into compati-
bility! But this would give only the Negative attri-
butes.[35]

Coleridge was never to find an auspicious moment to
evolve and expand this hint, though in his criticism of
Wordsworth's poetry he distinguishes between "words used
as the *arbitrary marks* of thought, our smooth market-coin
of intercourse," and words which convey pictures, "either
borrowed from *one* outward object to enliven and particular-
ize some *other;* or used allegorically to body forth the inward
state of the person speaking; or such as are at least the exponents of his peculiar turn and unusual extent of faculty."[36]
There are other hints scattered throughout his criticism
which show Coleridge's interest in the stylistic manipulation
of words, but obviously he had a profounder conception of
the function of language. This conception I find well expressed by a modern philosophical critic, Jean-Paul Sartre:

For the poet, language is a structure of the external
world. The speaker is *in a situation* in language; he is

[35] This notebook is still in the possession of the Coleridge family. The extract
quoted here is printed in Snyder, *op. cit.,* p. 138.
[36] *Biographia Literaria,* II, 98.

invested with words. They are prolongations of his meanings, his pincers, his antennae, his eyeglasses. He manoeuvres them from within; he feels them as if they were his body; he is surrounded by a verbal body which he is hardly aware of and which extends his action upon the world. The poet is outside of language. He sees words inside out as if he did not share the human condition, and as if he were first meeting the word as a barrier as he comes toward men. Instead of first knowing things by their name, it seems that first he has a silent contact with them, since, turning toward that other species of thing which for him is the word, touching them, testing them, palping them, he discovers in them a slight luminosity of their own and particular affinities with the earth, the sky, the water, and all created things.[37]

[37] From *Qu'est-ce que la littérature?* (1947). Trans. by Bernard Frechtman in *Partisan Review* (Nov.-Dec., 1947), p. 570. As for the "testing" and "palping" of words, cf. the following passage from the manuscript *Logic*: "In disciplining the mind one of the first rules should be, to lose no opportunity of tracing words to their origin; one good consequence of which will be, that he will be able to use the *language* of sight without being enslaved by its affections. He will at least secure himself from the delusive notion, that what is not *imageable* is likewise not *conceivable*. To emancipate the mind from the despotism of the eye is the first step towards its emancipation from the influences and intrusions of the senses, sensations and passions generally. Thus most effectively is the power of abstraction to be called forth, strengthened and familiarized, and it is this power of abstraction that chiefly distinguishes the human understanding from that of the higher animals — and in the different degree in which this power is developed, the superiority of man over man chiefly consists." Cf. Snyder, *op. cit.*, pp. 126-7.

That is an observation that Schelling, no less than Coleridge, would have found very sympathetic, and perhaps it is to be expected that a modern existentialist should speak the same language as one of the earliest exponents of existentialist philosophy. I realize that it may cause some surprise to hear Coleridge described as an existentialist, but I think it would not be difficult to justify the label. The origins of existentialism are usually traced to Kierkegaard; but a much better case can be made out for Schelling, as Dr. Bolman has already pointed out.[38] No doubt Coleridge was here again in debt to Schelling, but there is an actuality and eloquence in his statement of the problem which suggests that he had discovered it for himself. Take, for example, the following passage from *The Friend*:

> Hast thou ever raised thy mind to the consideration of existence, in and by itself, as the mere act of existing? Hast thou ever said to thyself thoughtfully, It is! Heedless in that moment, whether it were a man before thee, or a flower, or a grain of sand, — without reference, in short, to this or that particular mode or form of existence? If thou hast indeed attained to this, thou wilt have felt the presence of a mystery, which must have fixed thy spirit in awe and wonder. The very words, — There is nothing! or, — There was a time, when there was nothing! are self-contradictory. There is that within us which repels the proposition

[38] *Op. cit.*, pp. 8n, 56n, 198n.

with as full and instantaneous a light, as if it bore evidence against the fact in the right of its own eternity.

Not to be, then, is impossible: to be, incomprehensible. If thou hast mastered this intuition of absolute existence, thou wilt have learnt likewise, that it was this, and no other, which in the earlier ages seized the nobler minds, the elect among men, with a sort of sacred horror. This it was that first caused them to feel within themselves a something ineffably greater than their own individual nature. . . .[39]

I cannot pursue these metaphysical speculations of Coleridge's much further; I must content myself with pointing out that, writing before Kierkegaard was born, Coleridge had already formulated the terms of an existentialist philosophy — the *Angst* or sacred horror of nothingness, the Abyss or "chasm, which the moral being only . . . can fill up," the life in the idea which "may be awakened, but cannot be given," the divine impulse, "that the godlike alone can awaken."[40]

[39] *The Friend*, III, 192.

[40] A further quotation from Essay XI of the third volume of *The Friend* (p. 202) will illustrate in still further detail the existential nature of Coleridge's philosophy: "The groundwork, therefore, of all pure speculation is the full apprehension of the difference between the contemplation of reason, namely, that intuition of things which arises when we possess ourselves, as one with the whole, which is substantial knowledge, and that which presents itself when, transferring reality to the negations of reality, to the ever varying frame-work of the uniform life, we think of ourselves as separated beings, and place nature in antithesis to the mind, as object to subject, thing to thought, death to life. This is abstract knowledge, or

Once again we have come to the frontiers of philosophy, but once again I must affirm that philosophy directed the course and determined the ends of Coleridge's criticism. It had been very tempting — it still is tempting — to assign to art a teleological function. Schelling, in his earlier works, had not hesitated to do this — to make art the copula or connecting link between transcendental being and human consciousness — only in the work of art could man make an objective representation of the nature of the supreme reality. But that, as Coleridge and indeed Schelling himself were quick to perceive, would lead to an identification of the moral and the aesthetic. I personally believe that the identification is still possible, but for Coleridge, as later for Kierkegaard, there was inherent in the human situation an ineluctable Either/Or. For Coleridge a "standpoint," or a "starting-post" as he called it, was a psychological necessity — a knot must be tied in the thread before we can sew, as Kierkegaard expressed it; and Coleridge, at an early age, had made his standpoint the Christian revelation. He had a horror of any kind of self-consistent system — that seemed to him merely a dialectical trick, a mechanical top spinning in nothingness, not touching the human heart:

> the science of the mere understanding. By the former we know that exist-
> ence is its own predicate, self-affirmation, the one attribute in which all
> others are contained, not as parts, but as manifestations. It is an eternal
> and infinite self-rejoicing, self-loving, with a joy unfathomable, with a love
> all comprehensive. It is absolute; and the absolute is neither singly that
> which affirms, nor that which is affirmed; but the identity and living *copula*
> of both."

The inevitable result of all consequent reasoning [he said], in which the reason refuses to acknowledge a higher or deeper ground than it can itself supply, and weens to possess within itself the centre of its own system, is — and from Zeno the Eleatic to Spinoza, and from Spinoza to the Schellings, Okens and their adherents, of the present day, ever has been — pantheism under one or other of its modes, the least repulsive of which differs from the rest, not in its consequences, which are one and the same in all, and in all alike are practically atheistic, but only as it may express the striving of the philosopher himself to hide these consequences from his own mind.[41]

These religious considerations were decisive, but they were linked in Coleridge's mind with aesthetic considerations. He had come to realize, from his investigations into the nature of dramatic poetry, that all dramatic effect was dependent on a tragic sense of life. "To the idea of life," he wrote in his essay on "Poesy or Art," "victory or strife is necessary; as virtue consists not simply in the absence of vices, but in the overcoming of them. So it is in beauty."[42] The wisdom in nature gave unity and perfection — the thought and the product were one; but since there is no reflex act, no element of consciousness of existence, so there could be no moral responsibility. But in man there is re-

41 *The Friend*, III, 204.
42 *Biographia Literaria*, II, 262-3.

flexion, there is freedom, there is choice. This not only makes man "the head of visible creation"; it requires him to impose upon the images of nature the categories of moral reflection — to make thought nature, and nature thought.

At this point we must stop, for there Coleridge stopped. He had discovered that "existence is its own predicate"; that the dialectic intellect is "utterly incapable of communicating insight or conviction concerning the existence or possibility of the world, as different from Deity." But he did not trace out the consequences of this discovery for his philosophy of art. It was left for Kierkegaard to pronounce the absolute Either/Or — *either* the aesthetical *or* the ethical. The final beauty, for Coleridge and Schelling no less than for Kierkegaard, was the beauty of holiness; but it was left to Kierkegaard to point out, eloquently, loquaciously, that in the state of holiness you have passed beyond the spheres of nature and of art and are in the sphere of freedom, of the ethical.[43]

Coleridge's critical activity debouched (I can think of no more appropriate word to describe the physical effect) into this ethical realm, and as we are on this occasion restricted to his aesthetical realm, we must now take leave of him. I have given regrettably little account of the *variety* of Coleridge's criticism — of the brilliance and range of his perceptiveness. But those are incidental features of his work which must be appreciated extensively — without the

[43] Cf. *Either/Or*, trans. W. Lowrie (Princeton, 1944), II, 229.

intermediation of a secondary critic. I have confined myself
to general aspects of Coleridge's criticism, because only in
that way can we realize the greatness of his achievement. He
made criticism into a science, and using his own experiences
and those of his fellow poets as material for his research,
revealed to the world for the first time some part of the
mystery of genius and of the universal and eternal significance of art.

# APPENDIX

It may be useful in a brief appendix to trace the subsequent history of that "poetic monism" which was first suggested by the *Critique of Judgment* and then more firmly outlined by Schelling. From the first it held many attractions for Coleridge. Coleridge "thought the *Kritik der Urtheilskraft* the most astonishing of all Kant's works" — an ambiguous remark recorded by Henry Crabb Robinson (*Diary,* Nov. 15, 1810). (Coleridge's alternating attraction and repulsion *vis-à-vis* any form of pantheism is amusingly illustrated in another entry in Crabb Robinson's *Diary:* "1812. Nov. 3 . . . He walked with me to A. Robinson's for Spinoza wh. I lent him. In the course of a few minutes while standing in the room, Coleridge kissed Spinoza's face at the title page, said his book was his gospel, &, in less than a minute, added that his philosophy was after all false. . . . Did philosophy commence in an *It is* instead of an *I am,* Spinoza would be altogether true. And without allowing a breathing space he parenthetically asserted: — 'I however believe in all the doctrines of Christianity, even of the Trinity.'") Coleridge's final reaction to Schelling is expressed in a marginal note on the *Briefe über Dogmatismus und Criticismus (Biographia Literaria,* 2nd edition, Appendix): "The more I reflect, the more convinced I am of the gross materialism of the whole system!" But meanwhile Schelling himself had been moving away from his neat monistic system of antitheses. He had broken with Hegel as early as 1806, and the subsequent development of his thought was largely a reaction away from Hegel's panlogism. Dr. Bolman remarks (*Op. cit.*, p. 35) that "it was not until after 1827 that Schelling precisely stated the difference. That difference has to do with Schelling's self-confessed change in attitude toward his own early philosophy of nature; and that change revolves round the concept of God. Of his own philosophy of nature prior to 1804, Schelling had said:

> God was that subject which remains *as* subject, victorious over all, which can no longer fall into the object; just this subject had passed through all nature, through all history, through the succession of *all* moments, from which it apeared only as the final result. This passing through was represented as a real movement (not as a progress in mere thought), represented even as real process. Now I can indeed conceive God as end and mere result of my thought, as he was in ancient metaphysics, but I cannot conceive him as result of an *objective* process.

Dr. Bolman further quotes Schelling as saying, "Real thought is that whereby something opposed to thought is overcome. Where one has only thought, and that abstract thought, for content, thought has nothing to overcome." Schelling had, in effect, isolated for the first time the problem which has remained basic in modern philosophy — the struggle between conceptual necessity and existential freedom. That Coleridge was fully aware of the same problem has been my contention in the foregoing lecture. Coleridge criticized the early Schelling on precisely the same grounds that the later Schelling criticized Hegel: that he tried to make pure thought or logic account for existence; and with such a rationalist conception one could never enter the realm of existence. "Hegel's formal approach to free creation ended, according to Schelling, in pantheism of the worst kind, in which God has no freedom but enters endlessly into process" (Bolman, *op. cit.*, p. 37), which is exactly Coleridge's criticism of Schelling.

These later speculations of Schelling's were continued by Kierkegaard and taken up again by Husserl, and are now the preoccupation of Heidegger, Jaspers, Marcel, Sartre, and other so-called existentialists. But in this note I am more concerned with the fate of Schelling's earlier "nature" philosophy, for it was by no means liquidated by calling it pantheism. It was given a new stimulus by the biological theory of evolution, and both Nietzsche and Spencer are to be reckoned among its renovators. But its most formidable restatement has been due to Bergson, whose ambition it was to unite biology with metaphysics, the theory of life with the theory of knowledge. It seemed to Bergson that a theory of knowledge (such as Kant's or Schelling's) which does not place the intellect in the general evolution of life "will teach us neither how the frames of knowledge have been constructed nor how we can enlarge or go beyond them. It is necessary that these two enquiries, theory of knowledge and theory of life, should join each other, and, by a circular process, push each other on unceasingly" (*Creative Evolution* [Eng. trans., 1914], p. xiv).

Personally, I retain a considerable respect for the work of Bergson, but for those who would prefer a more up-to-date treatment of the whole subject, I can recommend the *Philosophie der Lebendigen Wirklichkeit* of Richard Woltereck. I believe that Professor Woltereck did not live to complete his work, and I have only seen the second volume of the trilogy he planned: *Ontologie des Lebendigen* (Stuttgart, Enke Verlag, 1940). It is not a work that I can read with any ease or understand with any certainty; but I can perhaps indicate its bearing on the problems which agitated Coleridge and still agitate all thinking men. Naturally, the ontology of a practical biologist like Woltereck cannot accommodate the irrational notion that "all true reality has both its ground and its evidence in the will, without which its complement science itself is but an elaborate game of shadows" (*The Friend*, III, 201). It is not quite clear what Coleridge meant by the "will" in this context, but he would certainly have regarded it as manifested only in human consciousness; whereas Woltereck assumes that will is inseparable from the life process, which, ever since its origin, has been "thrown back on its own resources, its own potencies, specific determinants (ideas), intentions and inner impulses, all of them subjective *powers* which are the immanent possession of concrete life-carriers." This is not just the materialism of a scientist opposed to all idealistic philosophies. Nor is it the familiar doctrine of vitalism, nor any kind of "panpsychism." The "genetic monism" of a single, progressive differentiation and intensification of life is opposed to the pluralism of "radically" different realities implicit in the somatic, psychic, and spiritual life forces. This new ontology tries to analyze the phenomenal characteristics of physical and more particularly living reality together with the objective, elementary characteristics lying behind them, and then to understand all these characteristics synthetically, as a whole. It insists that reality is one progressive flow of events, from which not only consciousness, but organic life itself has been disengaged or particularized — "life is a jump-like intensification of not-life, dying is a jump-like relapse into this prior form of reality." Attention is focused on *"the continuous fact of anamorphosis*, the single total event leading *upwards* from the elementary physical states of cosmic nebulae to a-biotic differentiation, then to simple and increasingly differentiated life, and finally to spiritual events, spiritual creativity and spiritual freedom."

Woltereck at this point opposes his view to Heidegger's. He admits that knowledge of existence implies certain "resonances," and that one of these is the "dread" arising from the consciousness of Nothing and the feeling of shipwreck that Heidegger has placed in the center of his teaching. But there is an equally valid and biologically more positive "resonance" which was first described by Aristotle — the amazement and wonder of the man awaking to contemplation and discovery, which is bound up with the inner urge to knowledge, in its turn a deepened and intensified form of "curiosity." This more positive "resonance" has associated with it a *joyfulness* and inner *impulse* to assimilate, examine, understand, create. The sciences as well as the arts are born of this impulse. All the high and genuine values which are expressed in art, or in love, or in the perception of truth, have their origin in this same impulse.

Nobody, Woltereck admits, can say which of these "resonances" has the more ontic significance for mankind as a whole: *the approach to transcendence* following on the feeling of shipwreck, or *the inward intensification* through some profound experience that transcends the ordinary sphere of self, an intensification coming from directly contrary feelings. This heightened sense of vitality in a man so gripped forms the *polar opposite* of the fundamental feeling described by Jaspers and Heidegger.

We can now return to Schelling and Coleridge and see that they were aware of both these resonances. There is plenty of Aristotelian wonderment in Schelling — the Schelling who said that "the best course of a life devoted to philosophy might be to begin with Plato and end with Aristotle" (*Sämtliche Werke*, II, 1, 380; quoted by Bolman, *op. cit.*, p. 39). As for Coleridge, his teleological enthusiasm is very evident in a passage like the following:

> In all interior things from the grass on the house top to the giant tree of the forest; from the gnats that swarm in its shade, and the mole that burrows amid its roots to the eagle which builds in its summit, and the elephant which browses on its branches, we behold — first, a subjection to universal laws by which each thing belongs to the whole, as interpenetrated by the powers of the whole; and secondly, the intervention of particular laws by which the universal laws are suspended or tempered for weal and sustenance of each particular class. Hence and thus we see too that each species, and each individual of every species, becomes a system, a world of its own. If then we behold this economy everywhere in the irrational creation, shall we not hold it probable that by some analogous intervention a similar temperament will have been effected for the rational and moral? Are we not entitled to expect some appropriate agency in behalf of the presiding and alone progressive creature? To presume some special provision for the permanent interest of the creature destined to move and grow towards that

divine humanity we have learnt to contemplate as the final cause of all creation, and as the centre in which all its lines converge?

There is further Coleridge's remark, in the essay "On Poesy or Art," on the essential interdependence of form and life: his express belief that living or life-producing ideas "are essentially one with the germinal causes in nature." There is again his statement that "the *rules* of the Imagination are themselves the very powers of growth and production" (*Biographia Literaria*, II, 65).

The importance of Woltereck's ontology is that it *reconciles* the rules of the imagination and the powers of growth which both Schelling and Coleridge increasingly felt to involve a contradiction, and which Kierkegaard presented as an inescapable dilemma. "The scientist," writes Woltereck, "who resolves to write or even to read an ontology is little inclined, but nevertheless *compelled*, to recognize a fact which he is wont to leave to psychology and philosophy and not acknowledge as belonging to his province. This is the fact that non-spatial, *inner data*, experiences of the INSIDE are just as real and just as important for knowledge as the "external" or material-extensive objects of our observation with the help of sense-organs and instruments. The ontology of INSIDE events investigates and evaluates the categorical experiences or internal events that are not reducible to other facts; we found such to be, for instance, *resonance* (in the form of dread, fear, amazement, rapture), and we can also cite the impulsion of the will to self-expression, furthermore let us say curiosity, the need of pleasure and value, the feeling of freedom . . . and various other internal facts the discussion of which we leave to the psychologist."

The resonance that impels us to self-expression and to what Woltereck elsewhere calls the highest capacity of all, *self-intensification,* certainly leads to the creation of both aesthetic and ethical values, and these are given the highest place in the teleological process. Woltereck's consideration of the many problems involved is much more nearly complete and much more complex than this note would suggest, but in my opinion his scientific approach to the fundamental problems of metaphysics has brought us in sight of that reconciliation of science and metaphysics which was one of Coleridge's, as it was one of Bergson's, dearest desires.

I should not conclude this note without acknowledging the help I have received from Mr. R. F. C. Hull, who has not only communicated his enthusiasm for Woltereck's work to me, but also put at my disposal some pages of translation that he had made for his own use.

*Henri M. Peyre*

# THE CRITICISM OF
# CONTEMPORARY WRITING

*A French View*

*Henri M. Peyre*

# THE CRITICISM OF
# CONTEMPORARY WRITING

## *A French View*

ANDRÉ GIDE, who, in his long and full life of almost four-score years, had never yet set foot on American shores, had agreed with enthusiasm to take part in the Symposium on criticism organized by the Department of Writing, Speech, and Drama of The Johns Hopkins University. He had spent part of the winter months in his Switzerland retreat, rereading Sainte-Beuve and Renan and meditating on criticism, which he had once called "the master quality of France and one in which she is incomparable." A heart ailment prevented, at the last minute, his transatlantic flight. The intimidating task of replacing him in a series of addresses from which French criticism could not well be absent fell upon a French professor in an American university who has, in a modest way, tried to be a critic as well as a scholar and a student of modern literary trends as well as one of past currents and of recognized masterpieces. Several of the views here expressed have been already presented in

my earlier writings, especially in *Writers and their Critics*
(1944). For permission to utilize some of the material first
gathered in that book, thanks are due to the Cornell University Press. To The Johns Hopkins University and those
who took the courageous initiative to call upon eminent
critics from this country and abroad to discuss a subject
often deemed alien to the pressing preoccupations of a
machine-haunted and war-ridden world, gratitude should
be voiced. "The rise of the critical spirit within a given
civilization is a symptom of health and maturity," wrote
Ludwig Lewisohn in 1932. If these words have any truth
in them, no era in the cultural history of America has been
healthier than the last twenty years.

For, parallel to the vitality and the almost primitive
energy lavishly and uncritically expended on the American
novel, short story, and poetry since the 1919 renaissance,
there has sprung up a movement of critical analysis which
has won the respect of the young and has given new life to
the understanding of literature in academic circles. Emerson, E. A. Poe, W. D. Howells, and Henry James had not
been lacking in critical acumen; and their pronouncements
or revelations on their taste and their art still command our
respect. Irving Babbitt, Paul Elmer More, J. E. Spingarn
had desperately tried to stem the tide of American letters
and to teach their ebullient contemporaries the validity of
a new humanism nostalgically built upon a Buddhistic inner
check, upon Aristotelian or Crocean standards. They have

in fact acted but little on the literature of their times, on which they systematically turned their backs. Huneker was too flamboyant and too versatile a discoverer of every new European iconoclast to exercise any lasting influence upon the creative writings of his own land, then attempting to strike roots in native ground. Only since the early nineteen-twenties has there been a series of independent yet well-concerted efforts on the part of American critics to re-examine the basis of literary judgment, to explore the mechanism of creation, and to clarify our views on values, standards, and the everlasting struggle waged in art between tradition and experiment. I. A. Richards, Kenneth Burke, and John Crowe Ransom, able logicians and psychologists; poets and acute analysts of poetry like Allen Tate and R. P. Blackmur; professors bent upon forcing poetical structure and imagery to render up their utmost secrets, like Robert Penn Warren and Cleanth Brooks; more traditional and perhaps more sensitive critics like Malcolm Cowley and Edmund Wilson; younger ones like Richard Bentley and Alfred Kazin: all have helped conquer for criticism a place of greater eminence and of higher respect among the literati than was ever before the case in the history of American, perhaps even of English, culture.

Yet the very quality of such an achievement invites one to point to some of its limitations. Complacency and the assumption of dogmatic infallibility would be conspicuously out of place when dealing with the branch of writing which, more than any other, is doomed to remain in a constant state of flux and to live dangerously near errors. The new criticism which has flourished since 1925 or so[1] has looked up to science and has borrowed from scientific method the best it can offer to literature: precision in its measurement, rigor in its definition of terms and notions, logical reasoning, respect for reality and for the intellect; it attempts to find an objective and when possible a fixed basis for critical judgment. At the very time when physical and biological sciences were seized with doubts about their own methods and their postulates of determinism and quantitative relations, psychologists, followed by many a critic, fanatically adopted the tests, the experiments, and the latent philosophy of science. I. A. Richards, in the earlier phase at least of his career, seemed to take for granted a behavioristic philosophy and treated psychology as differing but little from laboratory physics. He owed much to the latest idols of our age, semantics and linguistics, and asked from the critics of the future an equipment that the critics of the past had innocently done without, "a command of the methods of general linguistic analysis." Poetry, on which recent criticism has almost exclusively concentrated, has been studied especially as a complex of "stimuli" to which the reader offers "responses," as does the pet animal of

[1] There naturally is, and should be, a "new criticism" every twenty years, and the newest one, when evolved by the younger generation of the men born around 1925, is likely to react against the scientific-psychological trend of our own age.

modern psychologists, the rat, when "exposed" to sex stimulants or to an appetizing crust of cheese. The pleasure of the amateur of verse was shown to be chiefly the intellectual and severe enjoyment of perceiving a half-concealed structure; a poem, apparently inspired, was in effect contrived like a machine and "integrated" or "well knit" like a mechanical bomb. Like an apple or a watermelon, it could be carved ingeniously by the scalpel of the new critic, who, in thus doing, triumphantly revealed its hidden structure, or gazed at the *disjecta membra* thus obtained with the awe that structural and geometric order inspires in our modern Puritan students of literature.

Many of our contemporaries, like their predecessors in the second half of the last century who erred most triumphantly when they climbed on the band wagon of science, seem to take it for granted that only some semblance of scientific definition and measurement can endow the judgment of literature with any stability. They naïvely refrain from asking whether such stability and uniformity in the opinions expressed by varied people of different ages on writers and artists is at all desirable. For the powerful appeal of philosophical speculation and of literary discussion to the young people is precisely due to the absence of any objective and therefore standardized truth in those provinces of man's intellectual life. Problems there are never solved, because they have to be formulated anew by each newcomer. "All problems," Santayana remarked in his

*Obiter Dicta,* "are divided into two classes, soluble questions, which are trivial, and important questions, which are insoluble." It is, moreover, an amusing fallacy to imagine that the data of science, on which psychology, semantics, and the "new" criticism hope to be solidly founded, are less impervious to fashion or to change than tides of taste and personal appreciation of art and literature. Education, therapeutics, mental hygiene, and the nascent and pompous science of sex behavior, like the explanation of genius through its ancestors, environment, and nervous mechanism, have never been submitted to such fickle and abrupt ups and downs than since they resorted to scientific data, hoping thus to gain firmness and prestige. A literary or musical genius of today may still remain a genius in the eyes of our grandchildren forty years hence; but the scientist of today is sure to be contradicted, amended, perhaps smiled at, by the scientists of tomorrow.

It would be foolish indeed to try to anticipate the judgment of posterity in our attitude to contemporary works. Our duty is primarily to our own times, and to take our calculated and honestly accepted risk with our own generation, discriminating among superficial appearances to concentrate on the deeper underlying trends. But we owe it to the remarkable group of critics who have lately won undisputed prestige to criticism written in the English language to offer a few questions and to chart some of the unexplored or neglected lands still confronting those who

have already explored much. My own angle of vision is that
of a Frenchman living in America, probably and half consciously wishing that some of the benefits derived by his
native country from a different literary and critical atmosphere be extended to the United States, realizing at the
same time that many faults of which French criticism has
often been guilty (partisanship, nationalist prejudices,
complacency, occasional unfairness, excessive tendency to
label and categorize) should be branded as unfit for export.
America has ceased to be a young country fearful of assimi-
lating men and ideas from abroad; her culture, her institutions have reached full maturity and as much homogene-
ousness as may be desirable. She is now in a position to
profit unreservedly from the enrichment that foreign points
of view may bring to her intellectual and social achievements, provided such points of view be understanding and
constructive, even while honestly critical.

*

"Criticism stands like an interpreter between the inspired
and the uninspired." This sentence of Carlyle should be
borne well in mind by whoever assesses the gains made by
recent schools of critics. A critic should above all be humbly
conscious of his duty to serve the creator and the public. He
is probably thus shut off forever from any aspiration to
true greatness. "Remember," Sibelius is supposed to have

said to a disciple, "that no statue was ever raised to a critic."
It may be, indeed, that the phrase "great critic" is a contradiction in terms. We would certainly be more than chary of
assigning the adjective "great" to any of the eminent critics
of France, from Sainte-Beuve and Taine to Faguet and Thibaudet. If Diderot and Baudelaire, Goethe and Coleridge,
probably also Aristotle, remain great for us in some of their
critical writings, their superiority comes from their genius
as it manifested itself in other fields of literary creation.
They did not try to judge systematically the works of their
contemporaries,[2] still less to interpret them so as to win a
larger audience over to the new talents. They were, in different degrees, theoreticians or philosophers writing on
literature.

Such a role, to be sure, is an important one; but we
question whether dutiful students of Aristotle's poetics, of
Coleridge's doctrine on imagination, of Baudelaire's art
criticism have proved any the keener or deeper for it as dis-
coverers and interpreters of the new talents which sprang
up under their very eyes. The most admired among the
recent critics in the English-speaking countries have also
been doctrinaires, rather than practitioners, of criticism.
They have concentrated on one of the functions of criticism
which consists in developing a body of ideas which may enable us to discern with more subtlety the elements of literary

---

[2] Baudelaire did it with extraordinary insight, but only occasionally; Aristotle's *Didascalia* we do not possess.

creation and of literary appreciation. They have analyzed artistic values, and the words designating them, with careful scrutiny; they have learned and taught how to read a book and, after plodding through several volumes of psychology and linguistics, how to read a page. They have helped us form more exact notions on the meaning of reason, imagination, fancy, symbol, myth, and ultimately on the meaning of meaning itself. They have revived among us some of the fanatical gravity with which seventeenth-century humanists discussed the rules of tragedy, the unities, terror and pity, the nature of the epic, form in the novel, the pattern of imagery, and the structure and versification of lyrical poetry. In a word, and this is no mean achievement, we know today much more about what literature is and should be, and we certainly understand the literature of the past, especially that of the Greeks and of the seventeenth and eighteenth centuries, better than our predecessors could ever do. An immense store of analytical penetration, of subtle delving into the mysteries of poetical creation and the processes of ambiguity, suggestion, and metaphor has been expended by modern critics.

But so much intellectual labor has not met with its counterpart, and if we know more on the psychology of composition, it is doubtful whether we have helped readers feel more intensely and love literature more ardently. Yet criticism should feel as well as understand, and feel with unashamed pride without having to wait for the condescending permis-

sion grudgingly granted by modern theorizers who, at the
end of several years of laborious investigation, discover that
cognitions and emotions are both valid in their own ways
and that literature, after all, has the right to deal with affective states and even to delight in illogic. It might shake off
its fascination with the august pronouncements of Aristotle,
Boileau, Dryden, Dr. Johnson, Matthew Arnold, and T. S.
Eliot and attack frontally some of the fresh works now being
produced. There has been overindulgence on our part in
what was once called by H. L. Mencken "the criticism of
criticism of criticism." There is now room for a little less
analytical dissection of works already analyzed by our
predecessors and for a little more boldness, for a little less
disserting about the "magical and synthetic power" dear to
Coleridge and for a little more actual use of our imagination. *"Comprendre, c'est égaler,"* according to an ambitious
French saying. A critic might certainly attempt to recreate
in himself some of the strange gifts which make poets wield
the language of metaphor, paradox, and ambiguity that he
delights to trace in their complex working and to recapture
some of the artist's inner fire which transmuted molten lava
into gold.

John Cowper Powys said pointedly in his *Suspended
Judgments* that "the chief role of the intellect in criticism
is to protect us from the intellect." Less paradoxically, we
would submit that the wisest use of our intellect should be
that which brings us to feel with greater  acuity and to ex-

perience beauty or truth "with an entire soul," as Plato recommended. Searching for standards and elaborating on criteria is a valuable and, in truth, a very elusive purpose for a critic; acquiring or refining his taste might be hardly less elusive and far more profitable and enjoyable. A system of aesthetics may be just as harmful to a judge of other people's writings as a system of poetics has repeatedly proved to be for poets, and a theory of the novel for novelists. Indeed, the quest for a master key applicable to those variegated effects caused by imagery, music, more or less closely knit pattern, and structure in the diverse achievements of poetry reveals not a little naïveté in professionals of the study of literature. It is likely to hamper in us the plasticity and readiness to espouse art forms different from our own and to enter with suspended disbelief into a creator's inner world, qualities which have distinguished the most gifted tasters of literary works: Hazlitt, Pater, Virginia Woolf, Gundolf, Curtius, Croce, Gide, Rivière, Du Bos. The following words, written *à propos* of Taine by the most philosophical and probably the most learned mind among the French critics of this century, might well arrest our attention: "The more theories there are in a work of criticism, the greater are its chances of being outgrown and quickly discarded."[3]

\*

[3] A. Thibaudet, in *Revue de Paris* (April 15, 1928).

More persons are practicing criticism today than ever
before, and most of them are persons with a superior intellectual equipment. The periodicals of countries like France
and Italy are filled with interesting discussions of writers,
past and present; not a few of the serious periodicals in
English-speaking countries[4] are also devoted to the definition
of literary values, but usually in a more high-brow and for-
bidding fashion, with a note of bitterness at their isolation
and of self-righteous pride at differing from the Philistine
who does not know what he ought to like and for what reasons.

Few, however, are the critics who remain in that profession and eventually accede to a position of authority from
which they can influence literature. Most of them will try
their hand at so-called creative writing, or be attracted by
editorial or radio work, by political articles, or by reporting.
Either the profession is too little rewarding economically
or too strenuous mentally, or else it requires superhuman
resistance to the peril of staleness and is not conducive to
happy maturation of taste and intellect; for a critic who
remains a critic for two or three decades, as Sainte-Beuve,
Sarcey, Faguet once did in France, seems to be an impossible
paradox in Anglo-American letters. The critic, who struggles
in the most eminent among our contemporaries in their

---

[4] *Criterion, Calendar of Modern Letters* in the twenties in England; then
*Horizon, Scrutiny, Bookman, Hound and Horn* around 1930 in America;
then *Southern Review, Kenyon Review, Sewanee Review, Accent,* and
many others in America.

youth, dies even younger than the poet in them, or chooses silence at an age when a poet or a musician undertakes his most ambitious compositions. Edmund Wilson, Malcolm Cowley, Waldo Frank, Mencken, G. J. Nathan have hardly fulfilled the brilliant promise of their early works, when it seemed as if they were destined to rule regally over their literature. John Middleton Murry, Edwin Muir, Desmond MacCarthy, even T. S. Eliot (who has not since 1930 repeated the fine critical performances of his articles on "Tradition and the Individual Talent," on the Elizabethan dramatists, on Dante) similarly seem to drop by the wayside when still in the prime of life. Is it that good criticism requires a freshness of perception that the acquiring of experience and the accumulation of knowledge can only blunt? Certain it is that the power of sympathy, essential in a critic, appears to wear off quickly and that a sense of wonder, which would restore to professional interpreters of literature the joy of admiration for what deserves it, is woefully lacking in our unromantic generation. It requires uncommon humility for a critic of forty or fifty to submit temporarily to works written by men his juniors by ten or twenty years and to assess such works detachedly. Such a critic is constantly tempted to take the work under consideration as a pretext to indulge in his own profundity.[5] Oscar Wilde

[5] Aldous Huxley wrote in *Music at Night and Other Essays* (Chatto and Windus, 1931), p. 51: "Critics are often intelligent people who happen to be philosophers or literary artists and who find it convenient to make the criticism of other men's work a jumping-off place for their own creativity."

amusingly called criticism the only civilized form of autobiography and defined the critic's primary aim as "seeing
the object as in itself it really is not." His paradox contained
more truth than he probably fancied himself.

The critic's realm may be roughly divided into three
provinces. The first is that of general comment on literature,
its purpose, its forms, its relations with other arts and disci-
plines, its technique, its contacts with other ancient and
modern literatures. Such generalities are not without their
perils; but they must be periodically revitalized through
the efforts of critics developing an intellectual climate in
which the creation and the appreciation of literature can
flourish. The second occupation of the critic is to write on
past literature, to acquire and impart to others a sense of
perspective, a consciousness of traditions, and a taste enlightened and purified by some familiarity with the best that
was thought and said before us. Every generation must,
thanks in part to the help provided by its critical leaders, see
the past with undimmed eyes and reassimilate it through an
active reading which enlivens its classics with the new life
that is instilled into them by new readers. The new critic,
like the medieval apprentice or the knight of old, proves
his worth by measuring himself against his important predecessors and showing through his own example that all has
not been said already on Plato, Cervantes, Shakespeare, and
Pascal. After all, great classics are the volumes which offer
the widest scope to the most varied kinds of criticism and

an infinite and patient capacity for surviving the pains taken with them.

But the critic's third province, strewn with the worst pitfalls, comprises the literature that is being written around him. There the untrained reader can hardly venture without guidance; he will be bewildered by the mass of works thrown at him with deceptive advertisements, duped by his own prejudices, hampered by his laziness in the presence of books requiring unusual contention of the mind. Yet, however difficult some of the new literature and art produced around him may be, he approaches it with pathetic good will; for he suspects that there stands the most truthful — distorted and magnifying, but all the more truthful — mirror to the baffling time in which he lives. That mirror is called Proust, Lawrence, Joyce, Kafka, Faulkner, Malraux. If he is faced with the retort that those recent works are too obscure for him as yet, he will not desist. Obscurity has never yet stopped attracting young men to difficult literature, nor most men and women to the mysteries of religion, metaphysics, and psychoanalysis. "We cease to wonder at what we understand," as goes an oracular utterance of Dr. Johnson. And few of us believe we shall understand Picasso, Mallarmé, and Joyce so thoroughly that we shall cease to experience pleasurable wonder with them. But the public has a right to insist that, if obscurity there be, it should be up to the critics to dispel it. And if deciphering the difficult new work can only be a slow and collective task, requiring several generations of acute minds and trained sensibilities, the sooner the task is undertaken, the better. Contemporaries of the new art and literature may help their own audiences, and their successors in the field of critical elucidation, if they do not hesitate to approach modern works with humility and yet with audacity. They enjoy sources of information that critics yet unborn will miss: living in the same age as the writer, participating semiconsciously in his preoccupations, his allusions, his general "frame of reference," and being able to question him, to hear him, to be rectified by him occasionally.

It is our contention that a critic worthy of the name cannot be content with formulating general views on the nature and mechanism of literary creation and with limiting his attention to writers of the past. He must also venture into the danger zone of new works as yet untried, apply on them his ingenious methods of text analysis, discover their relations with the traditional currents in which they will be inserted, but also perceive them in their newness and originality. To refuse this task or to fulfill it with too glaring inadequacy is, in our eyes, tantamount to confessing that the would-be critic is not equipped with the lucidity and the courage which are the primary requisites of his profession.

The most common way of dodging the issue is, for the professor or critic faced with new works on which he is asked to express an opinion, to declare that time alone can tell and to refer the impatient reader to posterity, alone capable of rendering a verdict. There are certainly a few valid arguments in favor of such a soothing belief. Some sources of information will be available to the biographer, the historian of manners, even to the literary historian, which are closed to contemporaries of the work just published. The fecundity of *Finnegans Wake*, of T. S. Eliot's *Four Quartets*, of Dos Passos's *The Big Money*, therefore the importance of these books in the literary evolution of their century and, as it were, as social phenomena affecting a large number of readers, will be more apparent in 2020 than it is in 1940. Their genesis will then have been elucidated by diligent study of sources and of currents, and their posthumous life will throw some light on their content. Our teachers and our disciples are often the only discerning judges we meet in life.

More important still, and very little explored (for histories of literary, artistic, and musical taste are, for all practical purposes, nonexistent), is the fact that an innovator has to create his own public and to mold the very taste which will enable future generations to borrow his own lens or to listen with his own ears. Wordsworth, whose best poems were outrageously vilified by the most respected of his contemporary critics, indicted those blind professionals of mistaken judgment in an "Essay" appended to the 1815 edition of his poems. He wrote in that essay an illuminating sentence, inspired in part by Coleridge: "Every author, as far as he is great and at the same time original, has had the task of creating the taste by which he is to be enjoyed." But how can this great and original author begin creating the new taste unless a few chosen readers first discover him with sympathy and convert others to their enthusiasm? And should not some of those discerning readers be found among the critics whom love of literature is supposed to inflame and who, wearied with the monotonous banality of many of the current volumes offered to their appetite, should be on the lookout for novelty and originality?

The honest truth is that, if posterity will know more about the writers of today than we do, it is also in danger of feeling their works less intensely. And the debate between the relative importance of knowing and of feeling is, and will always be, an open one. In spite of their occasional pompous utterances, claiming that they are erecting for centuries to come *monumentum aere perennius*, poets and novelists, and of course dramatists and musical composers, are writing for their own time. Only if their time fails them will they, with some bitterness, throw their pens into the sea. We occasionally exclaim: "How wonderful it must have been to see *Hamlet* in 1602, to read Donne's love poems in the same year, or to live in England in some *annus mirabilis* of literature such as 1819, or in France in 1857 when great works by Michelet, Taine, Hugo, Flaubert, Baudelaire appeared within a few months!" Alas! Those who then could enjoy the masterpieces of those times either ignored them or vituperated against them when they had to read them as critics. And if, as is likely, similar great works sometimes see the light among us, we prefer to nod our heads disapprovingly, reluctant to admit that, as Keats's line says, "Great spirits now on earth are sojourning."

The appeal to posterity, like many of our errors of judgment, rests on a false analogy: that one sees a mountain or a picture better if one stands back with the proper perspective and that posterity alone, agreeing unanimously in its judgment on past works, provides us with the fixity which, in matters of taste, is devoutly wished by the fickle creature called man. How far, however, one must withdraw from the trees to see the forest better, or from the canvas to perceive its effects, remains a matter of uncertainty. As to stability, it fortunately has no place in matters of taste, or even in man's intellectual history. The posterity of Donne, of Pope, of Shelley, of Tennyson changes its mind on the greatness, or the relative eminence, of these poets every thirty years. The posterity of Meredith, Hardy, Galsworthy, Stendhal, Flaubert, and Loti, like that of Wagner and of Tchaikovsky, of Bouguereau, the *douanier* Rousseau, and Cézanne has uttered contradictory decrees within our own memory. Are we right today on Góngora, Maurice Scève, George Herbert, whom we extol, or were our predecessors right forty years ago? Is the baroque contemptible as was thought half a century ago, or sublime as we assert nowadays? And even if a reputation like Shakespeare's has victoriously survived a hundred and fifty years, the reasons for which Coleridge and Hazlitt, then Arnold and Pater, A. C. Bradley, T. S. Eliot, and Granville Barker have admired *Macbeth* and *A Winter's Tale* are so different, if not antithetic, that one wonders about the desirability of a unanimous verdict of posterity. "Dante will always be admired," Voltaire once remarked, "because no one ever reads him."

The truth is that posterity will be made up of men and women just as fallible and just as prejudiced as ourselves, or as those contemporaries of Wordsworth and Shelley, Stendhal and Baudelaire, Berlioz and Hugo Wolf, who saw nothing but incomprehensible lunacy and gross immorality in the works of those great men. If genius today is ahead of us, it will be just as much ahead of the young people of 1980, for they will hardly be more cultured or contemplative than we are; they will be even more distracted by the inventions which will by then have multiplied the subtle means of torture called *radio* and *television* and the skillful instruments designed to keep our minds from thinking called the *movies* and the *press*. We are ourselves probably not markedly cleverer than the contemporaries of Bach or of Beethoven, of Delacroix or of Monet, who failed to perceive the originality of those artists. If it be true that only a handful of men in each generation are capable of understanding the great talents living among them and that these happy few gradually convert others, while the fools passively adopt the judgment of the literati, it is all the more imperative that critics should be among those happy few. If they would write discriminatingly and with some depth on the works of their contemporaries which they select as the important ones appearing today, the reputation of those men would begin at once instead of having to wait in purgatory for fifty years.

And not a few errors might be redressed, or avoided. For it is too placidly reassuring indeed to admit that the conclusions of posterity are infallible: that on the one hand stand the great writers, who will receive henceforth a full chapter in histories of literature; on the other the minor writers are forever aligned, who will be enumerated in hurried paragraphs. Shakespeare, we are told, towers above Ben Jonson, Middleton, Ford, and Webster. Donne far outstrips all the other metaphysicals. Goethe and Schiller are the giants of German literature around 1800. Balzac and Stendhal alone deserve the rank of classics among the French fiction writers of 1800-1850. Such assertions, and many similar ones, are hardly ever challenged, and we deplore it, for passiveness and lazy conformity enter into our acceptance of certain works as classics, and of some writers as first-rate, while others are only to be second- and third-rate, like grocery products labeled by the salesman. But if the difference between the "great names" of poetry, music, painting, and the less great ones is what posterity conveniently takes it to be — an abyss, and a difference in nature, not in degree — is it conceivable that it remained unnoticed by most of the contemporary critics of Balzac, Beethoven,

Cézanne, Mallarmé, Schiller, Blake, Keats? It is high time that professionals of the history of literature and the arts be shaken out of their complacent acceptance of the ranks assigned by so-called posterity; and it would be just as timely for critics to profit from the innumerable mistakes accumulated by their predecessors and to examine the literature and arts of their time with a keener eye for the complex, elusive, and yet authentic ensemble of virtues and faults which goes by the name of greatness.

\*

France is often regarded as the chosen land of criticism. Such a compliment, if it is one, can be accepted by a Frenchman only if it is paid to the conscious spirit of self-criticism which has often driven French writers, from Montaigne to Gide and from Ronsard and Racine to Mauriac and Sartre, to express interesting views on their art, to stress design and form in their works, and to restrain the ebullience of an inspiration impatient of limits. Ideas on literature have been rife in France ever since the end of the Middle Ages and have granted literature a place of supreme, probably excessive, importance in French life. The Renaissance produced several arts of poetry; dissertations on the art of writing history, even on the art of the novel, and chiefly on tragedy and epic poetry flourished in the seventeenth century. In the eighteenth, a vast number of men with keen and independent minds (Fontenelle, Trublet, Du Bos, Diderot, etc.) launched original literary ideas on which the romantic movement was to feed: they submitted key words like genius, taste, imagination, poetry, the sublime, the beautiful to a powerful analysis. Yet few of the men who thus devoted themselves to thinking on literature reached true eminence as systematic critics appraising the heritage of the past and the works produced in their day: not even Boileau, Fénelon, and Diderot, the greatest of them all. It is a source of constant wonder for us today to watch the frailty and the occasional preposterousness of the judgments uttered by contemporaries, and often by their successors, on Rabelais, Ronsard, Scève, Corneille, Racine, Rousseau.

With the nineteenth century, the divorce between criticism and contemporary literature became even sharper. Yet the new relativist spirit introduced by the romantic revolution, the broadening of taste caused by the discovery of several foreign literatures, and the multiplication of the number of critics due to the spread of culture should then have favored the development of criticism. I have shown elsewhere, I believe,[6] that all the important writers of the period were gravely misunderstood by contemporary criticism. Even those whom we fondly view today as crystal-clear, rhetorical, and almost commonplace, traditional, moral, neoclassical, impeccable devotees of their art were charged with ob-

---

[6] In the volume mentioned above, *Writers and Their Critics* (Cornell University Press, 1944).

scurity, unnecessary difficulty, jargon, neglect of style and grammar, immorality, decadentism; and, worst of all accusations, they were pronounced unworthy to be French. Such were the compliments paid by critics to the early (and often the best) works of Lamartine, Vigny, Hugo, Stendhal, Balzac, George Sand, Michelet, Flaubert, Baudelaire, Zola, Rimbaud, Verlaine, Mallarmé, and later to Gide, Claudel, and Proust. The list of critics thus mistaken, blind, prejudiced against greatness when that greatness was new, or incapable of the mental effort that originality imposes upon the reader, is not composed of minor names and petty, untrained minds, caviling at writings that they cannot equal. It includes almost all the most influential and respected critics of the French nineteenth century: Sainte-Beuve, Jules Janin, Cuvillier-Fleury, Nisard, Saint-Marc Girardin, Paul de Saint-Victor, Caro, Barbey d'Aurevilly, Doudan, Taine, Pontmartin, J. J. Weiss, Schérer, Brunetière, Faguet, Lemaître, Anatole France, *et al.*

The only critic in the nineteenth century in France who hardly ever erred when passing judgment on his contemporaries was Baudelaire. Being only occasionally a critic of literature, he was not obliged to comment on the whole of contemporary production. But no wise critic should ever attempt such an unprofitable task; there is no dearth of great subjects and of important authors where he can practice his skill. *"L'insecte doit bien choisir son chêne,"* as Barbey d'Aurevilly scathingly said of the diminutive commentator shrewd enough to choose the hero through and with whom he will escape oblivion. From Baudelaire's prose works a few reflections might be culled which provide the best possible advice for critics, far more piercing than the precepts offered by more methodical and more obtuse professionals of criticism. But those reflections are no recipes: for Baudelaire lacked standards, never followed a methodical approach, and eschewed all system. A system, he said, "is a kind of damnation which drives us to a perpetual abjuration; one must unceasingly invent a new one, and thus endure cruel punishment."

A system brings indeed warm comfort to the intellect; it provides one with clear-cut reasons for one's judgments and with a convenient standard that we pull out of our pockets when in a quandary to ascertain how erratic is the new work which fails to come up to our measurement. Better still, a system, be it of criticism, of aesthetics, or of political thought, is certain to occupy an enviable place in histories of literature, art, or government: with delight will the historian expound the logical sequence of the systematic thinker, take its mechanism to pieces, then display his own cleverness by refuting it. But the ravage caused by systematic intellects in criticism lies before us. The worst errors of judgment have usually been caused by the critic's obstinate blinkers when he shut himself up in the dungeon of his preordained theory and lost his ability to enjoy new works which did not readily fall into his tyrannical rules or his neat pigeonholes. Again, Oscar Wilde's epigram is here apposite: "There are two ways of disliking art; one is to dislike it; the other is to like it rationally."

The two most important such critics, with an ax to grind and a doctrine which afforded them a vantage point from which to survey the literary flux, were, in France, Taine and Brunetière. Both were passionately sincere men endowed with uncommon reasoning powers and an oratorical style, and both deserve our respect. But their mistakes were legion. On Brunetière's heavy-handed defence of the theory of evolution, clumsily applied to literary genres, and on his stubborn condemnation of all that was not in conformity with the classical ideal, it would be too easy to expatiate: although he awoke many minds, often through provoking them to contradictions, he remains a minor critic. Taine was a man of greater stature. This agnostic was one of the most ardent believers who ever professed allegiance to reason.[7] His philosophical system on literary and artistic criticism will long be discussed in histories of literature, but his practice as a critic gives the lie to his theories. For if he wrote with vigor, in his youth, on Balzac and Stendhal and generalized

[7] He wrote in his youth to his intimate friend Prévost-Paradol: "I see, I believe, I know . . . I cannot but believe, since all kinds of certainty, logical, psychological, metaphysical, unite to strengthen in me the certitude in which I am at rest." Much later, in his old age, he uttered the beautiful and touching cry: "I believe everything is possible to human intelligence." The best utterances of Taine on his system of criticism are to be found in his *Letters*, more *nuancé* than his famous prefaces, especially those of April 29, 1864, to Havet; of May 17, 1864, to Cornélis de Witt; of May 30, 1864, to Sainte-Beuve.

with talent on English literature, he was deficient in the flair which, alone, helps a critic discover and appraise new writers. The Goncourt brothers went so far as to liken him to a perfect pointer or a hound who would lack only one organ: a nose. He could not bring himself to like even the realistic novelists who owed much to his theories: Flaubert, Daudet, Zola. He failed to understand Baudelaire, Verlaine, and the great poetical movement which, under his very eyes, broke away from the romantic school. In English literature, he, who reached manhood at the middle of the century, labeled as decadent Rossetti and Swinburne, ignored Browning, misunderstood Tennyson, but ranked Macaulay's speeches above all he had read since Pascal and *Aurora Leigh* above all the poetry written in England since Byron. At the age of forty or thereabout, he, like many other men, ceased to venture among the hazards of new writing; he pulled his carriage away from the train and let it rest on some comfortable track, as so many of us do when we reach the dangerous crest of the middle of our lives, and he turned from criticism to history to explain why his country and the world were falling into decay.

Opposed to such systematic critics stand men of greater subtlety who occasionally had the good fortune to utter perspicacious or prophetic judgments, since they dared contradict themselves and trust their instinct. They are Montégut, then Lemaître, Anatole France, and two keen adepts of the dissociation of ideas, Remy de Gourmont and Faguet.

They were once avidly read, and much feared. Yet the picture they offer us of French literature between 1840 and 1900 arouses a smile on our lips today. The most celebrated of all French critics, the saint and martyr of his profession, Sainte-Beuve, has been even less discerning on practically all the great figures of his age. He was occasionally biased by personal motives such as spite, rivalry, malice; more often, alas! he failed out of mere inability to perceive and praise what is truly great. He did not give their due to Chateaubriand (although he studied him in a separate work and in several articles), Lamartine, Hugo, Vigny; he was blind to Baudelaire's originality and recommended young Verlaine not to follow in the footsteps of that poor misfit, the author of *les Fleurs du mal*. Meanwhile he praised Béranger and Ponsard and wasted his attention on even more mediocre poets. He was likewise blind to the originality of Balzac, Stendhal, Mérimée, Flaubert, while he lauded cheaper novelists like Charles de Bernard and Feydeau. He stubbornly underrated and even reviled Michelet and Tocqueville. In a word, our present ranking of the French writers of 1800-1850 stands in glaring disagreement with that proposed by the critic who was their contemporary and their observer. Most of the *Lundis* devoted to his own age by Sainte-Beuve are dead today; and even the others show the critic eschewing the frontal attack on literary works, seldom uttering penetrating new truths on Pascal, Racine, and Voltaire. He preferred to take refuge in biography, amorously depicting the genesis and gradual formation of the man who was some day to compose great works and stopping short before those works; or else he shirked literary judgment through writing on historical figures, often obscure ones, whose memoirs and letters provided him with evidence on men and manners of past ages but did not provoke aesthetic pleasure.

Interest in the past and coolness toward the present would not in themselves deserve our censure. But Sainte-Beuve was not an antiquarian disclaiming interest in the literature of his contemporaries. Repeatedly, he asserted the duty of the critic to venture among new publications. The mere stocktaking of past achievements was loudly condemned by him in a famous passage written in 1831:

> There is another sort of criticism, more alert, more involved in the sound and fury of the day, lightly armed as it were, and ringing a signal for contemporary minds. . . . It must single out its heroes, its poets; it must attach itself to them, surround them with its loving advice, boldly throw at them the words of glory and of genius which horrify some spectators, fill with shame the mediocre creatures who rub their elbows against them, make room around them like the herald at arms, advance in front of their chariot like an outrider.

Later still, in 1860, in the final chapter of his *Chateaubriand*, Sainte-Beuve redefined as follows the function of the critic:

Anyone is competent to decide on Racine and Bos-
suet. . . . But the sagacious keenness of the judge, the
perspicaciousness of the critic are chiefly displayed in
his dealing with new writing, not yet tried by the public.
. . . The true critic anticipates the public, judges at first
sight and guides. . . . The gift of true criticism has been
bestowed on a very few. That gift even amounts to
genius when, amid revolutions of taste, ruins of an
older order crumbling down and innovations being attempted, one must distinguish with precision, certainty
and firmness what is good and what will live; decide
whether, in a new work, faults are redeemed by true
originality.

Such passages show that Sainte-Beuve, like many other
critics who failed to exhibit discrimination or, harder still
and even more desirable, to prophesy in judging the productions of their own time, suffered in fact from an evil con-
science. They realized that one probably does not understand the past aright if one fails to understand the present;
for the qualities of adventure, of bold vigor, and of revolutionary thought and technique which characterized the important authors in the past must be perceived by the critics
as such, and not as traditional virtues on which he discourses
without recreating them in himself. Those great men once
created a tradition; and the duty of criticism today is to recapture and appreciate, not the tradition as it is handed
down to us in half-dead form, but the spirit of courageous

and calculated risk which created the tradition by gambling against the routine and prejudices of its own age. A young and promising critic remarked, after visiting an octogenarian American in Italy and admiring the learning and taste of the old man, one of the most influential writers on art of this century: "I miss in him that quality which alone makes a thinker interesting: his commitment to the living."[8] Allen Tate, who cannot be accused of ignoring the great ancient and Western traditions but has repeatedly fought for living literature, chided the timid professor in his *Reason and Madness*: "The scholar who tells us that he understands Dryden but makes nothing of Hopkins or Yeats is telling us that he does not understand Dryden." Matthew Arnold himself, whose fame rests on a few felicitous formulas and on some general statements on the value of literature and the function of criticism rather than on the profundity of his analysis of individual writers, asserted:

> To ascertain the master-current in the literature of the epoch and to distinguish this from all minor currents, is one of the critic's highest functions; in discharging this, he shows how far he possesses the most indispensable quality of his office: justness of spirit.

A beautiful definition of the lofty standard to which a critic should aspire! Alas! Arnold fell signally short of it. He advocated the models of French and German culture before

---

[8] The words are by Alfred Kazin, "From an Italian Journal," in the *Partisan Review* (May, 1948), p. 559.

the "Philistines" of his native island; but he never felt
French poetry[9] and overrated many of the prose writers
whom he introduced to English readers from France, while
he praised Goethe's poetry for the worst possible reason:
"What is really deeply and fundamentally effective [in it]
. . . is what remains of the poet when he is translated into
prose." On his own compatriots, Pope and Dryden, he found
no higher compliment to bestow than calling them "classics
of our prose." He preferred the letter writer in Shelley to
the "ineffectual angel" and musician waylaid by poetry (!),
and insisted upon ranking Byron above both Coleridge and
Keats. His own generation counted at least six poets of eminence besides himself: Tennyson, Browning, Meredith,
Swinburne, Morris, and Rossetti. He gleefully ignored them
in his criticism. No wonder that one of his successors in the
Oxford chair of poetry, H. W. Garrod, had to confess in
1931 that Arnold's criticism "is tainted with a certain snob-
bery and even dandyism" and was always conceived by the
dutiful son of the Rugby schoolmaster as "a part of the
church service." Some twenty years earlier, Lytton Strachey,
ushering in the anti-Victorian reaction in criticism, scathingly remarked in his *Characters and Commentaries* that

> Arnold might, no doubt, if he had chosen, have done
> some excellent and lasting work upon the movements
> of glaciers or the fertilization of plants, or have been

[9] Molière excepted; "by far the chief name in French poetry," he calmly
declared in his *Irish Essays and Others*!

quite a satisfactory collector in an up-country district in India. But, no, he *would* be a critic.

\*

Such a lamentable succession of mistakes made by the most reputable critics of several lands, and the even more lamentable abdication of those who dodged the issue of appraisal of their contemporary literature, rightly arouse our anger. For they have injured literature itself. There exists no recipe for the creation of masterpieces; but some understanding criticism might have helped gifted artists and authors to avoid not a few blemishes in their works. A critic who accepts their vision, enters into their world, judges them according to their own laws, points out their occasional lapses from their own standards, suggests sympathetic and constructive improvement, can do much for a creator of talent, and occasionally for one of genius. Boileau when counseling his friend Racine, Rivière and Du Bos in our day, have not proved unworthy of such a delicate role. We believe that, however passionate and sensitive creators may be — a privilege they share with those other sensitive and passionate creators, women — they are also capable of occasional humility and of honest detachment. Keats would not have rejected understanding criticism of his *Endymion* or even of his *Hyperion*; Flaubert was most receptive to what Taine and Renan might say of his later novels; Baudelaire anxiously appealed for such judgment on his poems, even if appreciation were tempered with some faultfinding; Hart Crane valued the verdict of friends like Allen Tate and Malcolm Cowley. Many an author realizes that he needs to be told by a sympathetic yet objective observer where he has missed and where he has hit right. Better still, such thoughtful and well-meaning criticism of contemporary works, if more widely practiced in the reviews and in the universities, would alleviate the gravest evil from which writers suffer in America: their tragic isolation. The esteem of their peers, the cheering talk about their work and their plans, the stimulant of technical and intellectual intercourse are lacking around them.

The only values left are therefore publicity and money. "We do not have great writers in America," Hemingway replied (falsely, we trust) to a German questioner in *The Green Hills of Africa*; "something happens to our good writers at a certain age." The "something" is clearly the all-powerful attraction of money, in the absence of other values which would be created or fostered by criticism. An Irish observer of the American literary scene[10] similarly remarked that the United States, unlike France and Britain, do not seem to possess an "organized critical enclave" which constitutes, for a writer, his number-one public. That small public, which never opens a *Digest* and is not dazzled by

[10] Seán o'Faoláin, "Getting at which Public?," *The Virginia Quarterly Review* (winter, 1948).

the price paid by a magazine or by the movies for a manuscript, is far less numerous than the number-two or -three
publics. But its prestige and influence are out of proportion
to its size. Hence the ambition of writers to satisfy its demands: they create characters with some intellectual complexity and write with art and refinement, while gifted
Americans like Erskine Caldwell, William Saroyan, John
O'Hara, James M. Cain, Damon Runyon, *et al.*, disregard
such values and aim at more brutal effects.

But the readers themselves are worse losers than the
writers for the lack of intelligent criticism to attract them
to living literature that they might and should read. Space
is niggardly meted out to literature in the leading monthlies,
and it shrinks with every decade. Certainly, no future historian of American letters between 1919 and 1949 will find
in *Harper's* or *The Atlantic Monthly* an accurate picture of
the literary life of those crucial thirty years. What was then
the importance of the rediscovery of Melville? What view
was held of E. A. Poe and Walt Whitman? What influences
from Proust, Gide, Thomas Mann, Dostoievsky, Joyce
proved most fertile on the American soil? Which among
the champions of the ungenteel tradition and the lost generation achieved the most enduring work? What is the balance
sheet of the new poetry that flourished after 1910 in little
magazines? Why did the attraction of Marxism and social
protest, rife around the early thirties, end in disillusion-
ment? Why was the action of World War II so slow in being

felt by younger literary talents? What sifting could the
thoughtful critical opinion of their contemporaries effect
among the works of Thomas Wolfe, William Faulkner, John
Steinbeck? These, and many such questions, do not seem
to occur to the editors of our leading magazines. But they
do occur to the minds of many a common reader who used
to find some of them at least touched upon in the *New Re-
public* or in *The Nation* of twenty years ago, and nowadays
he has to resign himself to living in a critical desert. *The
Saturday Review of Literature* seems hardly conscious of
the role that it might have played, and half ashamed to prove
worthy of its title and to treat literature as such. Meanwhile,
the high-brow reviews published in academic communities
are so intent upon elaborating their critical methods and
refining the psychological jargon for designating mysterious
organic, ironic, and metaphorical devices of past poetry that
they forget to write articles discovering and appraising the
poetry which, an unheard melody around them, begs for a
sensitive audience.

The reading done by the average American is probably
not far inferior to that of the middle-class British and pro-
vincial French family, which is paying it a dubious tribute.
Cheap novels abound in middle-class homes all over the
literate world; and elevator boys, French concierges, dutiful
German petty officials have seldom been known to feed on
high-brow fiction. But the people who read trash in Western
Europe usually do so with the touching consciousness of their

inability to tackle the higher sort of writing that they know they should like. Literary or semiliterary weeklies, and even dailies, which reach the masses, tell them of the new books which are ranked as the best by the "elite"; a poet like Paul Valéry may be enigmatic and Claudel may be occasionally bewildering, but the man in the street holds them in respect. Gertrude Stein once remarked that, in France, if a shopkeeper whose merchandise is scarce or a garage employee whose space is crowded has to choose between a senator, an army general, a banker, and a writer, he will give priority to the writer, especially if the latter is a member of the French Academy. Gustave Lanson, alluding to a mediocre but extremely popular novelist, Georges Ohnet, whom the critic Jules Lemaître had flayed in a witty article, hinted that people probably continued to read him after the masterly critique, but never again dared confess it. Would that the readers of much of our detective fiction, which has now won devotees even among artists and professors, were similarly ashamed of their vice and disguised their weakness even if they must privately indulge in it, thus paying to virtue, that is to good taste, the homage due it by hypocrisy! But mediocre historical novels, standardized volumes written with an eye to the passivity of Book-of-the-Month Club subscribers (one dares not say "readers," for the monthly selections are more often prominently displayed in the living room than actually opened), lay sermons peppering Christian ethics with Freudianism and promising peace of mind or a well-adjusted love life often make up the only reading matter purchased by men and women who once went through college. As to poetry, when any is published by the leading monthlies and quarterlies (even by those connected with a university center), it is timidly inserted between two long prose articles so as to appear innocuous and seems to have been selected by superannuated devotees of Longfellow and Edna St. Vincent Millay. Meanwhile, the reading public is deprived of one of the most potent means of knowing and sensing the world in which it lives, of the keenest tool for understanding men's behavior, motives, and aspirations: literature.

\*

But must we despair, and concede that a young country, bent on creating a mass civilization and on democratizing culture, cannot aim at subtle discrimination among works produced in its midst; or assume that the gift of criticism cannot well coexist with the typical American qualities of vitality and exuberance? Such an answer would in our eyes be groundless and defeatist. Critical spirits like Henry James and T. S. Eliot were after all American, even if they eventually fled to other shores, as did Edith Wharton, Bernard Berenson, and George Santayana, acute masters of humor and of analysis. Soul searching has never been lacking in the country of Emerson and of the New England Puritans, nor among the Semitic elements of the population, renowned for their lucid talent for dissociating ideas (Ludwig Lewisohn, Waldo Frank, Alfred Kazin). Our own experience has often caused us to admire the superior quality of the critical essays written on their own writers and on foreign writers by the best American undergraduates. A present college population of two million young men and women, or of a million and a half in more normal times, constitutes a reservoir of critical talent and of appreciation of literature and the arts which remains untapped, for lack of confidence in our possibilities.

We need, first of all, more attempts at criticism by the writers and artists themselves. We are naturally not unaware of the peculiarities surrounding such criticism: it often amounts to an apology for their own talent by the writers, or on the contrary to envious praise of the gifts which are not theirs (Baudelaire lauding Balzac's and Hugo's imagination and facility, Gide coveting the hold on the concrete of Defoe and Fielding, the even flow of Conrad and Proust). But even such a "civilized form of autobiography" is revealing, of the models distortedly portrayed as well as of the painter. American writers are also capable of objectivity. Some of them are conscious artists and clear-sighted readers of their predecessors and of foreign works. If the criticism written around them were not superficial and standardized as it is in the more popular magazines, or hopelessly formalistic as it tends to be in the more specialized journals, our age might hope to reconcile its creators to a kind of writing which would bring them relaxation from their usual labor and win to them a refined audience. Henry James's "The Lesson of Balzac" is as valuable as at least half of his short stories. Robinson Jeffers has once or twice written strikingly on his conception of poetry, defending it against a renascent euphuism or Gongorism. We would give much for an appreciation of Mérimée or Verga by Hemingway, for some essays by O'Neill on Greek and English drama, by Faulkner on Balzac's *Human Comedy* or on his reading of Elizabethan writers.[11] And we believe that, if reviews convincingly asked for such essays from American writers, they would often secure them. Others still, like Thornton Wilder or Wallace Stevens, well-read and half-scholarly artists, could be expected to give us literary and critical essays at least equal in importance to their creative productions.

But we need, especially, more important criticism by the critics themselves. America has had, since 1910 or 1919, the most energetic group of writers of any country. But it seems obstinately unaware of it, because criticism has failed to play its part of elucidation and interpretation. Where are the important essays and volumes that Faulkner's talent would have inspired in any other country? The technique of Dos Passos has been discussed at length in France and treated as epoch-making, whatever the shortcomings of the

[11] Obviously, an essay by Faulkner or by O'Neill would not be detached, objective, learned, and dull like a professor's essay. But it might be more alive and illuminating. D. H. Lawrence's *Studies in Classical American Literature* far outweighs any other book on the subject, debatable as Lawrence's views and assertions may be.

use made of it by its inventor. Here magazines remain uninterested in reappraising *Manhattan Transfer* or *U. S. A.* Hart Crane has only now (in 1948) been studied in a careful critical monograph by Brom Weber. Many other poets in this great age of American letters are never comprehensively treated in reviews or books, and the average American can only marvel skeptically at the attention that the rest of the world grants the literature produced in his own land, of which nothing is ever heard in Middletown or on Main Street.

. Three conditions have to be fulfilled for such criticism to exist. There must be an important living literature on which to write, and we believe that there is little question on this score. The second condition is a large cultured public which should be and might be gained to a better appreciation of this literature: if such an audience is not to be found in a country which sends four hundred thousand students to college every year and millions to high school, we had better despair of our educational system and of our democracy altogether. A third factor is of importance: money with which to found the periodicals in which criticism of contemporary literature may appear. There again, if the rich men and the foundations in the United States, extraordinarily generous with gifts to encourage science, medicine, social studies, research in foreign relations, in anthropology, and in psychology, cannot be brought to take any interest in the living literature of their own country, something is radically deficient in our culture. And intelligent and combined efforts should be made without delay to awaken the "ruling classes" of America to the value of literature and of criticism.

\*

A fourth requirement must be added: there will have to be critics competent to undertake appreciation of the contemporary literature, and encouraged to do so. Since the potential talent is here, in the young men being trained in the universities and in many others outside who may fear the sterilization that academic work as conceived at present produces, we believe it would supply the demand if such demand arose, or were stimulated; in other words, if subsidized periodicals or publishers asked for the desirable articles. It is a sad reflection on the two richest nations in the modern world, the United States and Great Britain, that they are the only ones in which critical talent must starve or be stifled. The remark made by F. R. Leavis in reprinting in 1933 a selection of articles published in a short-lived English review (in *Towards Standards of Criticism*) unfortunately holds good for the American scene, too: "It is certain not merely that no good critic can now hope to make anything like a living by the exercise of his talents, but that he will be lucky if he is allowed to employ them in public at all."

But some truths (such they appear to us to be) may also be formulated anew to revitalize the critic's ideal, methods, and function. We should in all humility propose them as follows:

I. No monistic explanation of letters and art is valid, no system is unshakable, no recipes can be learned once for all. For literature does not consist solely of poetry, as our recent dissectors of poetry, never venturing to apply their subtle gifts to fiction or the drama, are apt to think, and poetry is not merely structure and metaphor. Subtlety is welcome, but so are common sense and the persistent reminder that analysis of art cannot be divorced from life. Literature involves everything in man: aesthetic sense, intellectual agility, but also moral values, philosophical outlook, religion. It can be great for a variety of contradictory reasons, and even for no palpable reason at all. The critic should remain ready to vary his approach with every author and every book.

II. Criticism involves even more: taste, in the most elementary meaning of the word. It is an affair of the emotions and of the senses: "Loving, and taking the liberties of a lover," as Virginia Woolf defined Hazlitt's gift as a critic. Before we dissect it, it is well to have experienced an emotion, even a thrill of pleasure at the contact of a new or eternal form of beauty. Then we may ask ourselves what is the quality of our pleasure, whether it is likely to be shared by others around us, or after us. Baudelaire called it, in a famous phrase: "to transform one's *volupté* into knowledge." And we may remind ourselves of the greater difficulty that we are likely to encounter in the greater works: for they demand of us that we submit to them more humbly and experience them more profoundly than ordinary books. "The qualities of a second-rate writer can easily be defined, but a first-rate writer can only be experienced. It is just the thing in him which escapes analysis that makes him first-rate."[12]

III. Criticism must be inspired, even as the work that the critic experiences and reinterprets. Only through a provoked yet ardent inspiration, and thanks to what Baudelaire regarded as the chief requisite of the critic, "passionate partiality," can the critic fuse himself temporarily with the creative process of the author. Such espousal may blur the scientific clarity of the judge for a moment; yet are not lovers or former lovers the most inflexible observers of their partner's weaknesses, once the marriage of minds and of souls has met with impediments? At any rate, such union with the impulse from which the great work originated will have brought the commentator, and his readers, closer to the book and its author. And any criticism which does not bring us closer to the work under consideration is, in our eyes, vitiated at the root. A French modern, André Suarès, who wrote some of the most impassioned aphorisms on the writers, painters, and musicians whom he loved, said: "Works of art are daughters of emotion. The critic's emotion must therefore equate that of the artist. Or else the critic is but a priest of nothingness."

12 Willa Cather, in her charming volume of critical essays entitled *Not under Forty*.

IV. Criticism must be open to newness and must constitute an adventure of the mind. It is too easy to rest content with seeking subtle mysteries in an elegy by Donne or in an ode by Wordsworth, or even to display one's vast scholarship by tracing all the allusions woven into *The Waste Land* and *Four Quartets*. It is a more challenging task to plunge into the *terrae incognitae* of literature, to sift the good from the chaos in current literary production, to clear avenues for our readers, to run chances of error, but to run them in good faith and with courage. "All great literature of the world has been the attempting of something new," wrote an Oxford professor who never lost his love for literature, Walter Raleigh, in *On Writing and Writers.* "It cannot be understood by those who see in it only an established model, who feel nothing of the original excitement of the poet." Past literature may gain from our reinterpretation, if we are men of unusual profundity, capable of reading in it secrets never yet perceived. But the forming body of literature clamors for our assistance; to it alone can we be of service. If we can claim any culture, thoroughness, independence of mind, and gift of discrimination, let us bring those accomplishments to the elucidation and judgment of recent works. For others will perforce criticize contemporary literature if we refuse to do it; and they are likely to be reviewers more hasty than ourselves, or untrained audiences practicing oral criticism with naïveté and superficiality.

V. A critic must feel, understand, and judge. He must

also communicate his experience and opinions to others: "What we have loved, others will love," in Wordsworth's phrase. The critic has not fulfilled half of his function if he has failed to win readers and recruit lovers to the work that he has admired. He should, therefore, be able to write and should cultivate his style so as to fire his readers with the enthusiasm that he first felt in himself. The scientific obsession of many a recent critic has led him to delight perversely in repelling his potential readers: he has beaten the laboratory physicist at his own game of abstruse terminology. In their anxiety to avoid the deluge of snappy vulgarisms into which authors of popular articles on literature believe they must plunge, scholarly critics have erected barriers of "objective correlatives," "organicity," and medical or psychological jargon at the door of their sanctum. Urbanity and charm, which never were the enemies of precise thinking and of sensitive perception, have disappeared from much contemporary criticism. As a result, only a few readers during a few years of their lives — while, as sophisticated college youth, they are seduced by labels and like to set themselves apart from the uninitiated crowd — can join the modern critics at their private game. It has apparently become old-fashioned to write with freshness and beauty on works of literature, that is to say, on things of beauty and of eternal freshness.

*

The critics whom we dream of seeing on the contemporary American scene are not paragons of ideal excellence whose coming would be a miracle. We are convinced that they exist potentially in our midst, and especially among the college youth: having lectured on three continents and in seven or eight countries, I feel justified in stating without flattery that the appreciation of literature is nowhere keener than in the American youth of both sexes. We are equally convinced that it would take only more financial support, more spiritual encouragement, and especially more faith on their part in their own possibilities, to recruit first-rate critics of modern art and letters from the ranks of American teachers and scholars. There need be no antagonism between the keepers of tradition and the accepters of new values, which very soon will in their turn be inserted into the tradition and become hardly distinguishable from it: Cézanne, so maligned in his lifetime, soon falls in line with Chardin and Poussin; Mallarmé, equally ridiculed, with Racine; and Debussy with a long series of French composers. Joyce and Stravinsky have joined the classics. If contemporary scholars choose to ignore genius and talent growing around them or to deride them because their newness baffles them, they are lacking in the first requisite of their trade: intellectual courage. An American professor reminded his colleagues of it some fifty years ago:

It is much safer to praise an old book than a new. . . . The old book has been duly labelled. Contempo-

rary merit is uncertain as yet; authorities have not
stamped it with their approval. A dull man gets a certain advantage over a clever man, if he is able to compare him, to his disadvantage, with some much cleverer
man who is already dead. . . . Some day his successors
will be lecturing their classes on the books now coming
out, just as he is engaged in expounding and interpreting authors whom time has made classic. But
scholarship has a Philistinism of its own and is not
always liberal in its reception of fresh talents.[13]

The American universities today rank among the very best
in the world. The faculties living on their campuses include
many of the finest brains in the country, the best informed,
the most disinterested. In other lands, their colleagues, or
men trained for the academic profession, have provided
many of the best writers of their age: Bergson, Péguy,
Romain Rolland, Jules Romains, Giraudoux, Maritain,
Sartre in France; the shrewdest critics of modern literature
in France at present are *agrégés* or otherwise academically
trained minds. Enlightened by the mistakes accumulated
by their predecessors, they have proved sympathetic to the
innovations of surrealism or existentialism, and yet discriminating interpreters and judges. Maurice Blanchot, Mme
Claude Magny, Gaetan Picon, Etiemble, Armand Hoog,
Roger Caillois, Thierry Maulnier, Mme Dominique Aury
are the most conspicuous names in that brilliant galaxy of

13 Henry A. Beers, in *Points at Issue* (Macmillan, 1904), pp. 44-45.

contemporary French critics who have dispelled the preju-
dice which long equated "academic" with "conservatively
and complacently severed from life." There is no reason the
same reversal of attitude should not take place, with clear
benefits both to the academic man and to the author, in the
United States. An attitude of starched dignity and pseudo-
scientific superiority has too often been assumed, doubtless
as an antidote to the vulgarity of many tabloid newspapers
and other paraphernalia of a mass civilization. Genteel
scholars have been repelled by the display of vitality in
Hemingway and Caldwell, the obsession of several American authors with drink and sex, their pessimism (in O'Neill,
Faulkner, and Jeffers), their cult of energy at the expense
of analysis and artistic refinement. They have failed to
realize that they were in part responsible for this morbid
insistence on vitality ("To be so preoccupied with vitality is
a symptom of anemia," according to Santayana, who, in his
middle eighties, produces a volume every year); for by
reserving their praise for distinguished but not very energetic talents like E. A. Robinson, Robert Frost, T. S. Eliot,
E. M. Forster, they have alienated the others and dug deeper
the ditch separating truly creative and often revolutionary
writing from the academic institutions.

It has become too easy and cheap to rail at Ph.D. theses
and professors' scholarly monographs. Some of the disre-
spect with which academic writing is received is, however,
justified. Too many volumes and articles thus produced fail

to impress one as having been written because the author *had* to write them, prompted by some inner necessity. "If people only wrote when they had something to say, and never merely because they wanted to write a book, or because they occupied a position such as the writing of books was expected of them, the mass of criticism would not be wholly out of proportion to the small number of critical books worth reading." Thus spoke a critic much admired by professors, T. S. Eliot, in *The Use of Poetry and the Use of Criticism*. Criticism is perhaps the least vital branch of writing in America today, partly because it has feared to take risks, as any inspired writing must. It has not fulfilled its function or its duty to literature, to society, to tradition. It has lacked imagination, sensuousness, energy, boldness, and, above all, continued contact with life and the power to communicate its faith with contagious and convincing enthusiasm. New methods, new psychology, and new semantics have brought their valuable contribution to modern criticism. But "old" sayings, such as this one uttered by George Edward Woodberry in 1907, have not ceased to be timely: "The secret of appreciation is to share the passion for life which literature itself exemplifies."

*Benedetto Croce*

# THE CONDITION
# OF CRITICISM IN ITALY

*Benedetto Croce*

# THE CONDITION
# OF CRITICISM IN ITALY

*Translated by Francis J. Thompson*

CRITICISM of poetry and art has had a very important history in Italy since the time in the Renaissance when Aristotle's *Poetics* and other treatises of the ancients were rediscovered. Their doctrines were then expanded, adapted, and made the object of fruitful controversies in the new poetry, literature, and art which were in full bloom. A learned American, whose premature passing we still lament, my friend, Joel Elias Spingarn, devoted one of his books to this period of criticism, and showed that these doctrines then became the poetic of all civilized countries, Latin and Germanic; and a German historian, Borinski, recognized independently that the Maestro of German criticism, Lessing, had based his work on that same source.

In spite of disturbed conditions in national politics, a weighty Catholic Counter Reformation, and the triumph of the baroque, in the following age the quick Italian genius continued to make progress in that field, forming new con-

cepts and opening new paths which are still quite serviceable
in modern thought. Among these was *taste* or *judgment of
sense,* an exact judgment, neither intellectual nor hedonis-
tic, which distinguished between the beautiful and ugly.
Another was *wit* or *genius,* the inventive or creative ability.
Yet another was *style,* the expression of the individuality
of the writer; and, above all, there was *imagination,* conceived to be the faculty proper to poetry and art.

Between the seventeenth and eighteenth centuries, the
treatises of Gravina and Muratori and the dissertations of
Calepio had considerable influence even outside Italy. Still
later, they worked upon the so-called Swiss School of Bod-
mer and Breitinger to such an extent that an English historian, Robertson, has traced the origin of romanticism to
these Italians. This is true, if it means by "romanticism"
the discovery of a more intimate meaning and a new dignity
in poetry. At the same time Vico, in his *Scienza Nuova,* with
philosophic profundity and rigor marked out the exact
place in the human mind which belongs to poetry, and to
language, which has its origin in poetry and song; and celebrated as supreme poets not Virgil and Petrarch, whose refined culture was preferred in the Renaissance, but the
genuine, powerful, though sometimes rude Homer and
Dante.

This tradition had its effect on Italian criticism and literary
history at the beginning of the nineteenth century, on Fos-
colo among others. Soon it entered into the aesthetic specu-

lations of Kant, Schiller, Schelling, Solger, and Hegel, and into the criticism of the two Schlegels and other German and Italian romantics.

Francesco De Sanctis gave birth to his theory in the middle of the nineteenth century amid these cultural surroundings, and worked among them for many years, selecting and rejecting, with fresh intuition and with a sure sense of what is the truth and reality of poetry. For such work he has been, and must be, recognized as the founder of the new criticism in Italy. And he deserved that his influence should spread through the culture of Europe, though it did not at that time. As early as the period between 1850 and 1860, De Sanctis had pointed out what the scope of the new criticism should be. He opposed two schools, the merits of which he recognized but which basically did not satisfy him: the German, which sought ideas in poetry and reduced it to philosophical dialectic, not realizing that the true importance of poetry is elsewhere, namely in its frank and a-philosophical representation of the human soul; and French criticism, which neglected or trespassed against poetry in order to make it a document of the emotional and everyday life of the writer. Against these two schools De Sanctis maintained that poetry is neither philosophy nor history, let alone biographical chronicle. It is the creation of aesthetic life. Similarly, he ruled out all the infinite and various disquisitions that had been toiled over for centuries and which were concerned with the theories and intentions

which poets held, or were supposed to hold, about their
"poetics" and their "ends." On the contrary, he insisted
on the essential point that poetry is not what the poet resolves, or thinks he has resolved to do. But it is only what
he really and successfully accomplishes in the poetic ecstasy
which inspired his song, of which he is sometimes unaware,
and which the reader and the critic must be able to relive.
And they do relive it and feel it again when, in reading a
poem, they yield themselves and gather the pure impression,
that is, the same image which was the end product of the
creative process of the poet. Anyone who fails to gather that
impression, anyone who loses it after having gathered it,
yet keeps on reasoning about art, inclines toward subtleties
and wearies himself in empty thoughts, because he has lost
the only compass that could have guided him. De Sanctis
proposed his doctrine in conformity with this and in spite
of the aesthetics of his own time, which in Germany above
all was notoriously productive of philosophical treatises,
setting "aesthetics of content" against "aesthetics of form,"
and finding no peace, because none could be found in eclec-
tic efforts to unify the two points of view. For De Sanctis,
aesthetics is, to be sure, form and nothing but form; but it is
not dead form separable from content or added to content
in a rhetorical way. It is what he called "living form," form
which overcomes the chaos which is its matter or abstract
content and makes it concrete by transfiguring it into the
aesthetic image.

De Sanctis had few followers except in Naples, where he taught. For it is a region singularly favorable to philosophizing, as Herder had already observed a century before, saying that "freedom of thought illuminates and favors the Bay of Naples." De Sanctis' words were re-echoed at first, but his thought was not thoroughly understood because no theory is truly understood except in the light of the critical judgment which continues and perfects it. When he put down his pen, the positivistic and antiphilosophic age was already in full bloom. Closed to the life of the spirit, it vainly sought truth where it could not be found, in the natural sciences. And contemporary with the European age of positivism, there was a "philologism" in the study of poetry and art. Even at its best the result of this was certainly not the understanding of poetry and art; it specialized in an acquaintance with the surroundings of art, in bibliography and the history of the fortunes of books, in searching for and editing texts to make them as exact as possible, in providing the biography of artists in their everyday life, in the formation and succession of their works considered extrinsically and not felt or understood aesthetically, and in other similar things. There arose, on the part of philologists, a scorn for De Sanctis, who was considered a dilettante and eccentric. They did not find him a colleague in their work, for such in effect he was not, and they could not understand that in him which departed so much from and was so far superior to and more complex than the sphere of their quite useful labors. A periodical entitled *Giornale storico della letteratura italiana* came into existence which is to be remembered because in its own province it was very important and worthy. It was opposed to what De Sanctis stood for in its very program, and proclaimed its forebears and masters (to whose examples it wished to return) to be Tiraboschi, Quadrio, and Crescimbeni, and such erudites of the eighteenth century. The journal still ekes out its life today, though disturbed and contaminated, even in its philological and bibliographical probity, by fascism, the corrupter and murderer of life, which twisted even that philological workshop to factious and wretched political propaganda.

The recovery of the tradition of De Sanctis became evident in the last years of the nineteenth century. It grew and waxed strong in the first half of our own century, with the resurgence of truly philosophical speculations as opposed to the hybrid variety of the natural sciences, puffed up into positivistic pseudo-philosophy. It was necessary above all to reduce to a rigorous and co-ordinated philosophical form that which De Sanctis had formulated somewhat aphoristically, and not without lacunae, uncertainties and with some contradictions. And this was achieved by interpreting the concept of "form," which he considered to be the queen of art, as an *a priori* synthesis of a Kantian type but of which Kant had not thought, a synthesis which, in analogy with the logical synthesis of judgment, is "empty without material (which is sentiment) just as sentiment is blind without category (which, in this case, is intuition)." This, therefore, may, from the categorical element which shapes it, be named briefly "intuition," a word which here designates the office or proper character of poetry and of art, and gives the definition of it which Kant did not succeed in giving in his *Critique of Judgment,* where art remains not a synthesis but an amalgamation of intellect and imagination. In De Sanctis, aesthetic form, which is made up of poetry, art, language, becomes the first act of frank and unreflecting cognition, and, for that reason, necessarily precedes the act of logic. Whereas in Kant what went before abstract and arbitrary judgment were the forms or, as he called them, the categories of intuition, space, and time that possess a different importance to the understanding and require the intellect. In De Sanctis, in addition to the absence of a methodical criticism of all other theories of art that had been proposed, there lingered residues of old distinctions which had been virtually, though not logically and expressly, surmounted by him. Among these were the long-standing distinction between the beautiful and art, where an identification should be made; the doctrine of literary genres, which should be rejected because it is extrinsically classificatory and not serviceable as a criterion either in artistic production or judgment; the doctrine of the specific character of each art; the relation between intuition and expression, which is one of identity, and so on; points which

were all re-examined and resolved in conformity with the
principle of intuition.

De Sanctis' idea of the history of poetry was also cor-
rected, an idea which, due to a certain Hegelian bent, showed
not a few traces of a dialectic of forms bound one to the
other by thesis, antithesis, and synthesis. But every poem is
an original creative process and for that reason demands a
monographic history which will tie it in securely with the
whole history of the human spirit, not merely with one or
several works of art. Thus an aesthetics, extensively developed and particularized, replaced the principles expressed
by De Sanctis. From these principles it received its original
impulse, and they are all contained in it, but placed in new
relations, better clarified and thought out, and enriched with
the many complements and consequences which they bear
within themselves, but which had not been deduced or not
well deduced.

Anyone who would like readily to know a great many of
these principles may refer to the book of the distinguished
American thinker, John Dewey, *Art as Experience* (1934).
By the spontaneous virtue of his acute mind, contrary to
the intentions of the author, this contains a good speculative philosophy (or "organic" philosophy, as he might
distastefully call it). Although Italian aesthetics does not
figure therein, except for a few rare critical allusions (which
I find not justified), in innumerable points it entirely con-
forms to the aesthetics which for half a century now has

been cultivated and is widely spread over Italy, as I showed in an article of mine when the book by Dewey appeared.[1] I say this, not in order to make the least protestation of priority, but only to point out the coincidence; because if Dewey came to these conclusions independently of Italian works in aesthetics (and that is something quite possible), I should be quite happy about it, as a spontaneous confirmation brought by him to the truth, which is all that matters.

It is also worth remembering that in Italian aesthetics the distinction between the concept of poetry and that of literature has been expressly treated, not in the usual manner, by considering literature as a kind of inferior or conventional or bad poetry; but, differentiated entirely from poetry, its own particular and proper character and value have been recognized. In poetry, content and form are one and the same thing: a poem cannot be "translated" into other words or rhythms without being destroyed or changed. But, in literature, aesthetic form dresses a content which may be expressed also non-aesthetically, in a phonic, graphic, or any other system of signs. Hence, for literature, the concepts of ancient rhetoric are valid, such as the distinction which is basic to those concepts, that of "bare form" and "adorned form." As distinguished from poetic genius, the positive function of literature is to respect and cultivate the aesthetic disposition of the human mind and to make

[1] It can be seen now in *Discorsi di varia filosofia* (Bari, Laterra, 1945), II, 112-113.

the two great wars, it penetrated more or less extensively
everywhere, and especially in England (where, among many
others, the sharp mind of Wackley, critic of *The Times,*
embraced and defended it); in Germany (where it was
effective in the formation of a new *Sprachphilosophie*);
and in the United States of America (where it found a
zealous champion, already mentioned, in Spingarn, who
published *The New Criticism* in 1911). Italian aesthetics
was translated even into Japanese, and also there found
disciples; and in the early years of the Bolshevik Revolution, when as yet a philosophy and a poetry of the state and
of the party had not been established, there was even one
who translated it into Russian.

But all this exceeds my theme, which was to inform you
of the condition of criticism in Italy; where, to conclude, I
should tell you that the school, which was formed in the
course of the first half of the century and is now in full
vigor, has been and is today opposed by current "hermetic"
or "stylistic" criticism, the younger sister of decadent "pure"
poetry.

This opposition actually offers nothing of any scientific
interest, although I have amused myself sometimes in com-
menting on the pronouncements of these critics in Italy. In
doing this, I do not know if I did well or not. Everyone has
his own temperament. I approve and admire the stern reso-
lution of my venerable ancestor Baumgarten, who baptized
the science which I foster and called it *Aesthetics.* In reply

to the stupidities which were being printed against his theory, misunderstanding and perverting his characterization of poetry as *oratio sensitiva perfecta* to *oratio perfecte* (that is, *omnino*) *sensitiva*, he prayed the Lord never to give him the time to *terere, dilapidare, perdere* in such disputes. But I, for my part, have not always found the calm to imitate him. In my turn I shall imitate him, however, by not causing you to waste time with such things.

*R. P. Blackmur*

# A BURDEN FOR CRITICS

*R. P. Blackmur*

# A BURDEN FOR CRITICS

WHEN George Santayana made his apology for writing a system of philosophy — one more after so many, one more after a lifetime of self-denial — he put his plea for forgiveness on the ground that he was an ignorant man, almost a poet. No doubt there was some reservation in Santayana's mind when he made that plea; no doubt there is some in mine when I adapt it to myself. This essay does not introduce a system of criticism; it is only a plea that criticism take up some of its possibilities that have been in abeyance, or in corruption, for some time; and it may be that like Santayana's philosophy it will look like an approach to a system. If so, it is the system of an ignorant man, and there is nothing in it that does not remind itself at every turn that it is the kind of ignorance which goes with being almost a poet. Poetry is one of the things we do to our ignorance; criticism makes us conscious of what we have done, and sometimes makes us conscious of what can be done next, or done again.

That consciousness is the way we feel the critic's burden.

By a burden, I mean both a weight and a refrain, something we carry and something that carries us along, something we have in possession and something that reminds us what we are. It is the burden of our momentum. In relation to it we get work done. Out of relation to it we get nothing done, except so far as we are swept along; and of course we are mainly swept along. The critic's job is to put us into maximum relation to the burden of our momentum, which means he has to run the risk of a greater degree of consciousness than his mind is fit for. He risks substituting the formulas of relation for the things related. I take it the critic is a relativist; but his relativism does not need to be either deterministic or positivistic, as in our time it usually is; he may rather be the relativist of insight, aspiration, vision. He is concerned with choice, not prescription, with equity not law; never with the dead hand, always with the vital purpose. He knows that the institution of literature, so far as it is alive, is made again at every instant. It is made afresh as part of the process of being known afresh; what is permanent is what is always fresh, and it can be fresh only in performance — that is, in reading and seeing and hearing what is actually in it at this place and this time. It is in performance that we find out relation to momentum. Or put another way, the critic brings to consciousness the means of performance.

*Perform* is a word of which we forget the singular beauty. Its meaning is: to furnish forth, to complete, to finish, in a sense which is influenced by the ideas clustered in the word

*form;* so that *performance* is an enlightening name for one
of our richest activities, rich with extra life. If it is the
characteristic intent of the critic to see about the conditions
of performance, it is his characteristic temptation to inter-
fere with those conditions. He will find substitutes; he will
make one condition do for every condition; he will make
precedent do for balance, or rote for authority; and, worst
of all, he will impose the excellence of something he understands upon something he does not understand. Then all the
richness of actual performance is gone. It is worth taking
precautions to prevent that loss, or at any rate to keep us
aware of the risk.

The precautions of the past come down to us as mottoes;
and for the critic of literature in our time I would suggest
three mottoes — all Latin — as exemplary. *Omnis intellectus omniformis est:* every mind is omniform, every mind
has latent in it all possible forms of the mind, even one's own
mind. The temptation is to make some single form of the
mind seem omnicompetent; omnicompetence becomes om-
niscience and asserts for itself closed authority based upon
a final revelation. *Omnis intellectus omniformis est.* This is
a motto of the Renaissance, and leads us directly to a motto
of the high Middle Ages, which preceded, or initiated, rather
than followed, an era of obsolute authority: *fides quaerens
intellectus.* If the temptation of the Renaissance was to put
one's own version of the mind in first place, the temptation
of the Middle Ages was to identify God with either one's

own knowledge of him or with one's particular form of faith. *Fides quaerens intellectus* is a motto meant to redeem that temptation; for it is faith alone that may question the intellect, as it is only the intellect that can curb faith. The very principle of balance, together with the radical precariousness of its nature, lies in the reversibility of this motto. Just so, the value of both these mottoes is heightened by putting them into relation with a third, which is classical in its time, and which has to do primarily neither with intellect nor faith but with the temptation of the moral sensibility. *Corruptio optima pessima*: in corruption the best is the worst. Here, in this motto, is that hard core of common sense — Cochrane's phrase — of which the Christian world has never got enough in its heritage from classical culture. It reminds the moral ego of its fatal temptation to forget that the ground it stands on is not its own, but other, various, and equal. Surely we have made the best in us the worst when we have either pushed an insight beyond its field or refused, when using one insight, to acknowledge the pressure of all those insights — those visions of value — with which it is in conflict. If we do not see this, we have lost the feeling of richness, the sense of relation, and the power of judgment; and without these we cannot, as conscious critics, bring our experience of literature to actual performance. We should know neither what to bring, nor what to look for.

All this is generality; it applies to literature chiefly in the sense that literature is one aspect among many of the general human enterprise. The horror, for critics, of most aspects of that enterprise is that they are exigent in action and will by no means stand still for criticism until they are done for. The beauty of literature is that it is exigent in the mind and will not only stand still but indeed never comes fully into its life of symbolic action until criticism has taken up the burden of bringing it into performance and finding its relation to the momentum of the whole enterprise. Both what constitutes performance and the very nature of relation — that is to say, what must be done and what may be taken for granted — change from time to time. It seems likely that one reason there has been so little great literature is that at most times so little has been required of it: how often has a Virgil felt obligated to create the myth of imperial culture? It is even more likely that the ability to cope with the task was wanting when required: how often has a Dante turned up to put into actual order all that had been running into the disorder of the rigid intellect and the arbitrary will? Ordinarily, past times have required little of literature in the way either of creating or ordering a culture. The artist's task was principally to express the continuity of his culture and the turbulence that underlay it. That is perhaps why we find the history of criticism so much concerned with matters of decorum: that is to say, with conformity, elegance, rhetoric, or metrics: matters not now commonly found or considered in the reviews. In our own time — if I may be permitted the exaggerations of ignorance and of poetry —

almost everything is required of the arts and particularly of literature. Almost the whole job of culture, as it has formerly been understood, has been dumped into the hands of the writer. Possibly a new form of culture, appropriate to a massive urban society, is emerging: at any rate there are writers who write with a new ignorance and a new collective illiteracy: I mean the Luce magazines and Hollywood. But the old drives persist. Those who seem to be the chief writers of our time have found their subjects in attempting to dramatize at once both the culture and the turbulence it was meant to control, and in doing so they have had practically to create — as it happens, to re-create — the terms, the very symbolic substance, of the culture as they went along.

I do not mean that this has happened by arrogation on the part of the writers; I mean they have been left alone with this subject as part of the actual experience of life in our time: which is always the subject which importunes every serious writer if he is honest and can keep himself free of the grosser hallucinations. The actual is always the medium through which the visitation of the Muse is felt. Perhaps a distinction will clarify what is meant. It is getting on towards a century since Matthew Arnold suggested that poetry could perhaps take over the expressive functions of religion. Possibly Arnold only meant the functions of the Church of England and the lesser dissenting sects. Whatever he meant, it did not happen, it could not and it cannot happen. All poetry can do is to dramatize, to express, what has actually happened to religion. This it has done. It has not replaced or in any way taken over the functions of religion; but it has been compelled to replace the operative force of religion as a resource with the discovery, or creation, of religion as an aesthetic experience. The poet has to put his religion itself into his poetry along with his experience of it. Think, together, of the religious poetry of George Herbert and of T. S. Eliot: of how little Herbert had to do before he got to his poetry, of how much Eliot is compelled to put into his poetry before he is free to write it. Consider too — and perhaps this is more emphatic of what has happened — the enormous mass of exegetical criticism it has seemed necessary and desirable to apply to Eliot's poetry and indeed to the whole school of Donne. This criticism neither compares, nor judges; it elucidates scripture.

Let us put the matter as a question. Why do we treat poetry, and gain by doing so, after much the same fashion as Augustine treated the scriptures in the fifth century? Why do we make of our criticism an essay in the understanding of words and bend upon that essay exclusively every tool of insight and analysis we possess? Why do we have to recreate so much of the poem in the simple reading which is only the preface to total performance? Do we, like Augustine, live in an interregnum, after a certainty, anticipating a synthesis? If so, unlike Augustine, we lack a special revelation: we take what we can find, and what we find is that art is, as Augustine sometimes thought, a human increment to creation. If this is so, how, then, has it come about?

We know very well how it has come about, and we come late enough in the sequence of our time so that we can summarize it in what looks like an orderly form — or at any rate a poetic form. It composes into something we can understand. We come late in a time when the burden of descriptive and historical knowledge is greater than any man or group of men can encompass; when the labor by which our society gets along from day to day is not only divided but disparate and to the individual laborer fragmentary; and when, in an effort to cope with the burden of knowledge and the division of labor, we have resorted to the adulterative process called universal education.

As a natural effect of such a situation we have the disappearance or at least the submergence of tradition in the sense that it is no longer available at either an instinctive or a critical level but must be looked for, dug out, and largely re-created as if it were a new thing and not tradition at all. We have also a decay of the power of conviction or mastery; we permit ourselves everywhere to be overwhelmed by the accidents of our massive ignorance and by the apparent subjectivity of our individual purposes. Thus we have lost the field of common reference, we have dwindled in our ability to think symbolically, and as we look about us we see all our old unconscious skills at life disappearing without any apparent means of developing new unconscious skills.

We have seen rise instead a whole series of highly conscious, but deeply dubious and precarious skills which have been lodged in the sciences of psychology, anthropology, and sociology, together with the whole confusion of practices which go with urbanization. Consider how all these techniques have been developed along lines that discover trouble, undermine purpose, blight consciousness, and prevent decision; how they promote uncertainty, insecurity, anxiety, and incoherence; how above all they provide barriers between us and access to our common enterprise. Perhaps the unwieldy and unmanipulable fact of urbanization does more of the damage than the conscious techniques.

But this is not a diagnosis; it is a statement of sequence, a composition of things in relation. At the point where we arrest this sequence, and think in terms of what we can remember of our old culture, does it not seem plain to us what we have? Do we not have a society in which we see the attrition of law and rational wisdom and general craft? Do we not have an age anti-intellectual and violent, in which there is felt a kind of total responsibility to total disorder? Who looks ahead except to a panacea or a millennium which is interchangeable with an invoked anarchy, whether in the world or in the individual personality? Do we not above all each day wonderfully improve our chances of misunderstanding each other? These are the questions we ask of a living, not a dead, society.

They become more emphatic when we ask them about the schools of art and criticism which accompanied this shift in the structure of society. If we begin with Arnold's effort at the secularization of the old culture, it is easy to remind ourselves of the sequence that it began. Here it is, in very rough order. The hedonism in Pater, the naturalism of Zola, the impressionism of Anatole France, art for art as of the nineties, the naturalistic relativism of de Gourmont, the aestheticism of the psychologists, the rebirth of symbolism (as in Mallarmé and Yeats), the private mind, imagism and free verse, futurism, expressionism and expressive form, Dada and surrealism, dream literature, spontaneous or automatic form, anti-intellectual form, the school of Donne in English and American poetry, the stream of consciousness (that libel on Joyce), the revolution of the word, the new cult of the word. Some of these phrases will carry different meanings to different people; let us say that the general sequence runs towards some kind of autonomous and absolute creation and therefore towards total literalism.

That is on the positive side. On the negative side, every school on the list except Arnold's secularism, which was less a school than a plea for one, is an attack on disinterestedness of mind and imagination, though none of them meant to be so. And Arnold, who meant just the opposite, helped them at their business by seeing too much necessity in the offing. All of them either accepted or revolted violently against a predetermined necessity; none of them was able to choose necessity or to identify it with his will. None of them was apparently acquainted with the sense of our Latin mottoes.

Their only causes were Lost Causes; their only individuals were atoms; they reflected their time, as schools must.

The world has about now caught up with these trains of ideas, these images, trends, habits, patterns, these tendencies towards either mass action or isolated action — equally violent whether in attraction or repulsion. It is a world of engineers and anarchs; rather like the Roman world when the impulse of Virgil and the Emperor Augustus had died out and the impulse of Benedict and Augustine had not yet altered the direction and aspect of the general momentum. It is a world alive and moving but which does not understand itself.

Of this world individual artists have given a much better account than the doctrines of their schools would suggest, and they have done so for two reasons. The arts cannot help reacting directly and conventionally to what is actual in their own time; nor can the arts help, whether consciously or not, working into their masterpieces what has survived of the full tradition — however they may contort or corrupt it. They deal with life or experience itself, both what is new and what is accumulated, inherited, still living. They cannot come *de novo*. They cannot help, therefore, creating at a disinterested level, despite themselves. That is why they constitute a resource of what is not new — the greater part of ourselves — and a means of focusing what is new, all that necessarily aggravates us and tears at our nerve ends in our friction with it. That is why Chartres Cathedral survives better than the schools of the Bishop of Chartres; though both were equally vital in their time.

Consider in this light what seem to be the masterpieces of our time. Consider the poetry of Eliot, Yeats, Valéry, Rilke; the novels of Joyce, Gide, Hemingway, Proust, Mann, Kafka; the plays of Shaw, Pirandello, O'Neill; the music of Stravinsky, Bloch, Bartók, Ravel, Satie, Schönberg; the painting of Matisse, Picasso, Rouault, Marin, Hartley; the sculpture of Maillol, Brancusi, Faggi, Lachaise, Zorach, Archipenko, Moore. Think also, but at another level, not easy to keep in strict parallel, of the architecture of Leviathan: the railway station at Philadelphia, the Pentagon, the skyscrapers, the gasoline stations, the highway systems, the East and West Side Highways, apartment houses each a small city, and the interminable multiple dwellings. Think too of the beautiful bridges which connect or traverse eyesores: the George Washington Bridge, the Pulaski Skyway. Lastly, for architecture, think of the National Parks, with their boulevards running at mountain peak.

What an expression of an intolerable, disintegrating, irrational world: a doomed world, nevertheless surviving, throwing up value after value with inexhaustible energy but without a principle in sight. And how difficult to understand the arts which throw up the values. Only Hemingway and Maillol in the roster above perhaps made works which seem readily accessible when seriously approached. Shaw is as difficult as Joyce, Mann as Kafka, if you really look into them. The difficulties arise, it seems to me, partly because of the conditions of society outlined above as they affect the audience and partly because of these same conditions as they affect the artist at his work. The two are not the same, though they are related. The audience is able to bring less to the work of art than under the conditions of the old culture, and the artist is required to bring more. What has changed its aspect is the way the institutions, the conceptions, the experience of culture gets into the arts. What has happened is what was said above: almost the whole job of culture has been dumped on the artist's hands.

It is at this point that we begin to get at the burden of criticism in our time. It is, to put it one way, to make bridges between the society and the arts: to prepare the audience for its art and to prepare the arts for their artists. The two kinds of preparation may sometimes be made in one structure; but there is more often a difference of emphasis required. Performance, the condition we are after, cannot mean the same thing to the audience and the artist. The audience needs instruction in the lost skill of symbolic thinking. The arts need rather to be shown how their old roles can be played in new conditions. To do either, both need to be allied to the intellectual habits of the time. Besides analysis, elucidation, and comparison, which Eliot once listed as the functions of criticism, criticism in our time must also come to judgment.

If we look at the dominant development in criticism in

English during the last thirty years — all that Mr. Ransom means by the New Criticism — with its fineness of analysis, its expertness of elucidation, and its ramifying specialization of detail — we must see how natural, and at bottom how facile, a thing it has been. It has been the critics' way of being swept along, buoyed more by the rush than by the body of things. It is a criticism, that is, which has dealt almost exclusively either with the executive technique of poetry (and only with a part of that) or with the general verbal techniques of language. Most of its practitioners have been men gifted in penetrating the private symbolisms and elucidating the language of all that part of modern poetry we have come to call the school of Donne. With a different criticism possibly another part of modern poetry might have become dominant, say the apocalyptic school — though of course I cannot myself think so. In any case, it was a criticism created to cope with and develop the kind of poetry illustrated by Eliot's *Waste Land* and Yeats' *Tower*, two poems which made desperate attempts to reassert the tradition under modern conditions: Eliot by Christianity, Yeats by a private philosophy. Eminently suited for the *initial* stages of criticism of this poetry, it has never been suited to the later stages of criticism; neither Eliot nor Yeats has been compared or judged because there has been no criticism able to take those burdens. For the rest, the "new criticism" has been suited for *some* older poetry, but less because of the nature of the poetry than because of the limitation of the modern reader. For most older poetry it is not suited for anything but sidelights, and has therefore made misjudgments when applied. It is useless for Dante, Chaucer, Goethe, or Racine. Applied to drama, it is disfiguring, as it is to the late seventeenth- and all the eighteenth-century poetry. Yet it has had to be used and abused because there has seemed no other way of recreating — in the absence of a positive culture outside poetry — a verbal sensibility capable of coping with the poetry at all. In a stable society with a shared culture capable of convictions, masteries, and vital dogmas, such a criticism might have needed only its parallel developments for the novel and the play and the older forms of all literature; such a society does not need much criticism. But in an unstable society like ours, precisely because the burden put upon the arts is so unfamiliar and so extensive (it is always the maximum burden in intensity), a multiple burden is put upon criticism to bring the art to full performance. We have to compare and judge as well as analyze and elucidate. We have to make plain not only what people are reading, but also — as Augustine and the other fathers had to do with the scriptures — what they are reading about.

Here I do not wish to be misunderstood. Critics are not fathers of a new church. I speak from a secular point of view confronting what I believe to be a secular world which is not well understood; and I suppose what I want criticism to do can as well as not be described as the development of aesthetic judgment — the judgment of the rational imagination — to conform with the vast increase of material which seems in our time capable only of aesthetic experience. This is not to define a revelation or create a society. It is to define and explore the representations in art of what is actually going on in existing society. I see no reason why all forms of the word *aesthetic* cannot be restored to good society among literary critics by remembering its origin in a Greek word meaning to perceive, and remembering also its gradual historical limitation to what is perceived or felt — that is, what is actually there — in the arts. I have here the company of Bergson, who thought that the serious arts gave the aesthetic experience of the true nature of what the institutions of society are meant to control. And in another way, I have more support than I want in the philosophy of Whitehead, who found that the sciences in new growth, far from giving us knowledge with relation among its parts, give us instead abstractions good for practical manipulation but conformable only to a mystery. As a consequence, his philosophy of organism, with its attribution of feeling relations everywhere, is an aesthetic philosophy: in which knowledge comes to us as an aesthetic experience.

We do not need to go so far as Whitehead. The sort of thing that is wanted here to go on with seems to show clearly in James Joyce, whose *Ulysses* is the direct aesthetic experience of the breakdown of the whole Graeco-Christian world, not only in emotion but also in concept. Or again, Mann's *Magic Mountain* is the projected aesthetic experience of both that whole world and the sickness which is breaking it down. And again, Gide's *Counterfeiters* is a kind of gratuitous aesthetic experience — a free possibility — of what is happening along with the breakdown. Lastly, Eliot's religious poetry is a partly utopian and partly direct aesthetic experience of the actual Christian life today. That is what these works are about, and they cannot be judged aesthetically until full stock has been taken of what they are about. For us, they create their subjects; and indeed it is the most conspicuous thing about them that they do so. On each of these authors — even Eliot in his kind of reference — the whole substance of his subject is a necessary part of the aesthetic experience of it. It is for that reason that we have to judge the subject as well as what is done with it. To exaggerate only a little, in the world as it is, there is no way to get a mastery of the subject except in the aesthetic experience. How do we go about doing so?

That is, how does criticism enlarge its aesthetics to go with the enlargement of aesthetic experience? Here we must take again the risk of generalization, and we must begin with a generalization to get what the sciences have done with aesthetics out of the way. If we do not get rid of them by generalization we cannot get rid of them at all, for in detail their techniques are very tempting. Let us say then that psychology turns aesthetics into the mechanics of perception, that scientific logic turns it into semasiology, just as technical philosophers had already turned it into a branch of epistemology. All these studies are troublemakers and lead, like our social studies, to the proliferation of a sequence of insoluble and irrelevant problems so far as the critic of literature is concerned. Let us put it provisionally, that for the literary critic aesthetics comprises the study of superficial and mechanical executive techniques, partly in themselves, but also and mainly in relation to the ulterior techniques of conceptual form and of symbolic form. I do not say that one of these is deeper or more important than another, certainly not in isolation. But let us take them in the order given, and generalize a program of work.

By superficial and mechanical executive techniques I mean the whole rationale of management and manipulation through more or less arbitrary devices which can be learned, which can be made elegant, and which are to some extent the creatures of taste or fashion so far as particular choice is concerned. In some lucky cases they may be the sole preoccupation of the working artist, as in some unlucky cases they may be the one aspect of his work to which he seemingly pays least attention. In our own day they are troublesome to the extent that they are ignored in an abeyance from which they ought to be redeemed. It would seem to me, for example, that a considerable amount of potentially excellent verse fails to make its way because the uses of meter — in the sense that all verse has meter — are not well understood, though they are now beginning again to be played with: Mr. Eliot has just resorted to the metrics of Johnson and Milton. The critic who is capable of doing so ought to examine into the meters of his victims. Similarly, the full narrative mode is in little use by serious novelists, and the full dramatic mode is not in much more use; yet these are the basic modes of a man telling a story. If only because they are difficult, the critic ought to argue for them when he sees a weakness which might have been turned into a strength by their use. Again, and related to the two previous examples, there is a great deal of obscurity in modern writing which could be cleared up if writers could be forced (only by criticism) to develop a skill in making positive statement, whether generalized or particular, whether in verse or in prose. Statement may make art great and ought not to be subject to fashion.

And so on. The critic can have little authority as a pedagogue. The main study of executive techniques will always be, to repeat, in relation to the ulterior techniques of conceptual and symbolic form. By conceptual techniques I mean the rationale of what the artist does with his dominant convictions, or obsessions, or insights, or visions, and how they are translated into major stresses of human relations as they are actually experienced. Here we are concerned with the aesthetics of the idea in relation to the actual, of the rational in relation to what is rationalized. In Dostoevsky, for example, we are interested in his conception of the Double only as we see what happens to it in the character of Versilov, or Raskolnikov, or Dmitri Karamazov. In

Joyce's *Ulysses* it is not the Homeric pattern of father and
son that counts, but what happens to the conception of in-
transigence in Stephen in concert and conflict with that
transigent man Bloom. So in the later poems of Yeats, the
concepts of the phases of the moon are interesting as they
work or fail to work in the chaos and anarchy and order of
actual lyric emotions. On a more generalized level, it is
through concern with conceptual techniques that one notes
that the European novels of greatest stature seem to follow,
not the conceptual pattern of Greek tragedy but the pattern
of Christian rebirth, conversion, or change of heart; which
is why novels do not have tragic heroes. But examples are
endless.

And all of them, as those just cited, would tend if pursued
to lead us into the territory of symbolic techniques which
underlies and transcends them. I am not satisfied with the
term. By symbolic techniques I mean what happens in the
arts — *what gets into the arts* — that makes them relatively
inexhaustible so long as they are understood. I mean what
happens in the arts by means of fresh annunciations of resi-
dual or traditional forces, whether in the language, culture,
or institutions of the artist's society. I mean those forces
which operate in the arts that are greater than ourselves
and come from beyond or under ourselves. But I am not
satisfied with the definitions any more than I am with the
term. It may be I mean invokable forces, or raw forces, the
force of reality, whatever reality may be, pressing into and

transforming our actual experience. It is what bears us and
what we cannot bear except through the intervention of one
of the great modes of the mind, religion, philosophy, or art,
which, giving us the illusion of distance and control, makes
*them,* too, seem forces greater than ourselves. It is in the
figure of Dante himself in *The Divine Comedy,* Faustus in
*Doctor Faustus,* Hamlet and Lear in *Hamlet* and *King Lear,*
Emma Bovary in *Madame Bovary,* all the brothers in *The
Brothers Karamazov.* It is in the conjunction of the gods of
the river and of the sea with the Christian gods in Eliot's *Dry
Salvages.* It is the force of reality pressing into the actuality
of symbolic form. Its technique is the technique of so concen-
trating or combining the known techniques as to discover or
release that force. It is for this purpose and in this way
that the executive, conceptual, and symbolic techniques go
rationally together: the logic, the rhetoric, and the poetic;
they make together the rationale of that enterprise in the
discovery of life which is art. But the arts are not life,
though in the sense of this argument they may make a
rationale for discovering life. Whether they do or not, and
how far, is the act of judgment that is also the last act in
bringing particular works of art to full performance. Because the arts are imperfect, they can be judged only im-
perfectly by aesthetic means. They must be judged, therefore, by the declaration and elucidation of identity in terms
of the whole enterprise that they feed, and of which they
are the play, the aesthetic experience. There is a confusion

here that cannot be clarified, for it is a confusion of real
things, as words are confused in a line of verse, the better
the line the more completely, so that we cannot tell which
ones govern the others. The confusion is, that it is through
the aesthetic experience of it that we discover, and discover again, what life is, and that at present, if our account
of it is correct, we also discover what our culture is. It is
therefore worth while considering the usefulness of a sequence of rational critical judgments upon the art of our
time as an aid in determining the identity, the meaning in
itself, of present society. Such a sequence of judgments
might transform us who judge more than the art judged.

Here, perhaps, is a good point to sweep some bad rub-
bish into the bins. Critical judgment need not be arrogant
in its ambitions, only in its failures. Nor is it concerned
with ranks and hierarchies, except incidentally. What I
mean by judgment is what Aristotle would have meant by
the fullest possible declaratory proposition of identity.
Again, the ideal of judgment — no more to be reached by
critics than by other men — is theological: as a soul is
judged finally, quite apart from its history, for what it really
is at the moment of judgment. Our human approximation of
such judgment will be reached if we keep the ideal of it in
mind and with that aid make our fullest act of recognition.
Judgment is the critic's best recognition.

Thus it is now clear that my purpose in proposing a heavy
burden for criticism is, to say the least of it, evangelical.

What I want to evangelize in the arts is rational intent, rational statement, and rational technique; and I want to do it through technical judgment, clarifying judgment, and the judgment of discovery, which together I call rational judgment. I do not know if I should have enough eloquence to persuade even myself to consider such a burden for criticism, did I not have, this time not as precautions but as mentors, my three Latin mottoes. *Omnis intellectus omniformis est. Fides quaerens intellectus. Corruptio optima pessima.* They point the risk, and make it worth taking.

RANDALL LIBRARY-UNCW

3 0490 0334886 5